The
Rosetta Stone

The
Rosetta Stone

ROBERT SOLÉ &

DOMINIQUE VALBELLE

TRANSLATED BY STEVEN RENDALL

FOUR WALLS EIGHT WINDOWS

NEW YORK / LONDON

2002

Published in the United States by
Four Walls Eight Windows
39 West 14th Street, room 503
New York, NY 10011
Visit our website at http://www.4W8W.com

Originally published as *La Pierre de Rosette* by Editions du Seuil, Paris 1999

Cataloging-in-Publication data for this book has been filed with the Library of Congress.

10   9   8   7   6   5   4   3   2   1

First printing April 2002
Printed in the United States of America

Credits for plates between pp 88 and 89

The fort of Abukir, A house near Rosetta, Hassan Kachef's palace in Cairo, The hieroglyphic inscription from the *Description de l'Égypte*, The demotic inscription, The Greek inscription: © Michel Sidhom, Institut d'Orient, Paris

A far-fetched explanation of Egyptian religion by Athanasius Kircher: Jean Vigne

Thomas Young; Antoine Isaac Silvestre de Sancy; Jean-François Champollion: Roger-Viollet
Edme François Jomard: © Bibliothèque centrale M.N.H.N., Paris

The Rosetta Stone after being cleaned in 1998: © Copyright the British Museum

A complete new edition of the text and plates of the *Description de l'Égypte*, with a new commentary on the plates, is available from Michel Sidhom, Institut d'Orient, Paris (www.institut-orient.com)

The text illustrations of pp. 11 and 43 are also © Michel Sidhom. The Kircher engraving on p. 19 is courtesy Jean Vigne.

The hieroglyph decorating the text is a modern version, by Peter Campbell, of the hieroglyph *sesh*, "write."

Contents

List of Illustrations

Acknowledgements

The authors are grateful to Mmes Christiane Desroches-Noblecourt and Fayza Haikal; to Jean-Yves Carrez-Maratray; Didier Devauchelle; Harry James; Henry Laurens; Jean Leclant; Maurice Martin; S. J.; Richard Parkinson; Naguib-Michel Sidhom; Jean Yoyotte; Alain Zivie; the Egyptian Department of the British Museum; Cabinet d'égyptologie du Collège de France; Bibliothèque de l'Institute français d'archéologie orientale du Caire.

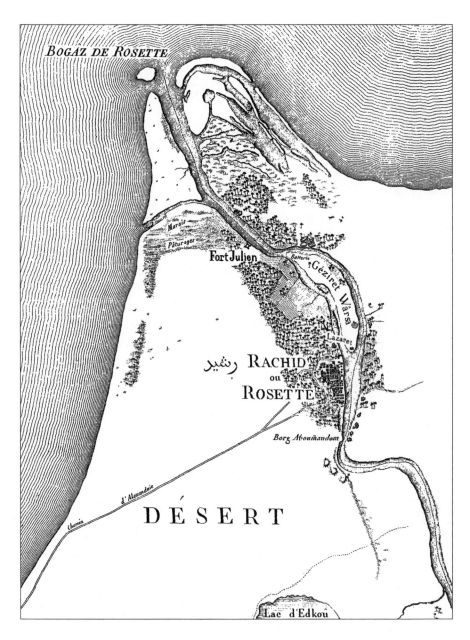

Detail of a map in the Description de l'Égypte.

CHAPTER ONE

Fort Julien

A RCHAEOLOGY? That was last thing on the minds of the
French soldiers occupying northern Egypt in July 1799!
Thousands of Ottoman invaders had just landed at Abukir –
that accursed place where the preceding year Napoleon's fleet
had been cut to pieces by the English. They had no difficulty in
taking the fort over which the French tricolour flew. The burn-
ing question was what their next target would be: Alexandria
or Rosetta?

In contrast to Alexandria, which looked like a large, dusty
village, Rosetta was an attractive and prosperous city. Situated
on the west branch of the Nile, a few kilometres from the
Mediterranean, it was green throughout the year. It was full of
banana, orange, fig and date trees, and had an abundant supply of pigeons and milk. Europeans thought it the most pleas-
ant city in Egypt.

North of Rosetta, fortifications were being hurriedly built
to resist a possible Ottoman assault. 'I expect to be attacked at
any time,' the local commander wrote to Napoleon on 18 July.
'I am vigilant and I hope the enemy will not take Fort Julien as
easily as he took the fort at Abukir.'[1]

'Fort Julien' was the *Borg Rashid* (the tower of Rosetta), a
dilapidated fortress built in the fifteenth century by the sultan
Qait Bey. The French renamed it in memory of one of
Napoleon's aides-de-camp, Adjutant-General Julien (spelled
'Jullien' in some military documents), who had been killed

nearby, along with his escort, the previous July.

Located in a palm grove on the east bank of the Nile, Borg Rashid was too far inland to control the entrance from the sea. However, from the fort an observer with the appropriate equipment could survey the whole breadth of the river's mouth, as well as the opposite bank. On taking it, the French found ruined walls eighty metres on a side, with four movable turrets in which not even an 'eight-pound cannon could be mounted'.[2] On the ramparts connecting the turrets, the crenellations were uncovered. The tower keep at the centre of the fortress contained a small mosque and two cisterns. Until more significant modifications could be made, they had hastily to adapt the turreted bastions and construct a terreplein bordering the ramparts. Living quarters, a hospital, ovens, guard units and ammunition dumps were set up, 'sheltered from bombs'. The establishment of this line of defence was entrusted to d'Hautpol, the leader of a battalion of engineers, assisted by Lieutenant Bouchard. History was to forget the former and immortalize the latter, by associating him with one of the most exciting scientific adventures of all time.

An officer-scientist

During the second week of July, while clearing away debris in part of Borg Rashid, Bouchard and his men found a block of dark-coloured stone about one metre in height. One of its sides, highly polished, bore thousands of small marks inscribed in three different scripts: the text on top was in hieroglyphs, the one on the bottom in Greek, and between the two were characters that could not be identified.

There was no reason for hieroglyphs to be found in an Arab fortress. Could the fortress have been built on the side of an ancient monument? Geographers were to declare this impossible, for in antiquity this region was covered by the waters of the Nile, which encroached much further on the dry land. All indications were that the stone had been erected elsewhere and brought to the site centuries later to be reused for other purposes. Later on, it would be proven that, like many of the decorated blocks used in the city's residences, it came from one of the temples in Sais, on the same branch of the river.[3]

Who was the first to see the Stone in the July heat? A soldier? An engineer? An Egyptian manual labourer? Who first cried out in surprise and realized that this might be a treasure? The official report attributes the discovery to Pierre François Xavier Bouchard, and there is no reason to doubt that this loyal and conscientious officer, who was then twenty-eight years of age and had always served the Republic much better than it ever served him, was the first European to set eyes on the Rosetta Stone. After all, Bouchard was a 'scientist': when the French first landed in Egypt a year earlier, he had belonged not to the army but to the Commission of Arts and Sciences, that is, to the group of some 160 civilians Napoleon had recruited to accompany his expedition. The discovery of the Rosetta Stone – by chance, in an improbable place and at an inappropriate moment – was at least made by a 'scientist' ...

The son of a carpenter, Bouchard was born on 29 April 1771 in Orgelet, a small village in the Jura mountains.[4] After completing his studies in Besançon, he was conscripted into the army, assigned to a company of grenadiers, and sent to the front in Champagne and Belgium. At twenty-three, this tall, dark man from the Jura, found himself in a new branch of the army: the *aérostiers*, an observational balloon corps that had performed with distinction in the battle of Fleurus. He soon became the assistant head of the aerostatic school established in Meudon under the direction of a brilliant inventor, Nicolas Jacques Conté, to whom we owe the artificial pencil lead. The two men were both wounded in a laboratory accident that left Bouchard with severely impaired vision in one eye.

In 1796, even though he had passed the age limit, the son

of the Orgelet carpenter was admitted to the recently established École polytechnique. Less than two years later, he decided, along with other students and several professors, to follow General Bonaparte on a lengthy expedition whose goal was kept secret. It was to be Egypt ... Bouchard took his final examination in Cairo and joined the engineering corps. He was not assigned to Rosetta until June 1799, a few weeks before the discovery of the famous Stone.

Three versions of the same text

The Stone was dusted off and sheltered, so that it could be closely examined. It weighed 720 kilos, and was 114 centimetres high, 72 centimetres wide and 27 centimetres thick on average. Its upper part was missing, as well as the lower right corner.

Although the Frenchmen then in Rosetta were unable to make anything of the first two inscriptions, they could read the Greek. They determined that it was a rather obscure expression of homage to a certain Ptolemy, written on the occasion of the thirtieth anniversary of his coronation. So far, nothing earth-shattering. It would interest only a historian of ancient Egypt ... But the last sentence excited them: 'This decree shall be inscribed on stelae of hard rock, in sacred characters, both native and Greek, and they shall be erected in each of the temples of the first, second and third category, next to the image of the king living eternally.' The stela contained the same text written in three different scripts! This opened a stunning perspective – starting from the Greek, wouldn't it be possible to decipher the hieroglyphics, which no one had been able to read for fourteen centuries? The importance of the 'stone with three inscriptions' seems to have been immediately perceived. A fine example of scientific intuition, even as the roar of battle could be heard close by.

What role should we attribute to Michel-Ange Lancret, who was assigned to the region around Rosetta? This twenty-five year old engineer, who had studied architecture before turning to mathematics, was in the first class to graduate from the École polytechnique. He had just been elected to the Institut d'Égypte created by Napoleon on the model of the Institut national. Lancret was a brilliant young man, but he lacked Bouchard's training in archaeology: he was simply one of the young 'scientists' who were open-minded and able to move beyond their own disciplines to take a passionate interest in something new. A year earlier, at the first session of the Institut d'Égypte, the mathematician Gaspard Monge, who presided over this scientific academy, had encouraged his colleagues to open their eyes and devote themselves 'to the study of ancient monuments, to explaining these mysterious signs, these granite pages on which an enigmatic history is inscribed.'[5]

It was Lancret who wrote a letter informing members of the Institute of the discovery of the stela, while Bouchard was entrusted with transporting it up the Nile by boat and bringing it to the capital. The Frenchmen in Cairo thus learned at the same time of the existence of the Rosetta Stone and of Napoleon's crushing defeat of the Ottomans at Abukir on 25 July. Both were good news – and news of great importance.

CHAPTER TWO

The thirty-first session

THE INSTITUT d'Égypte met twice a month in the palace of Hassan Kashef, one of the sumptuous homes in Cairo that Napoleon had requisitioned to lodge his scientists and artists. Its thirty-first session took place on 11 Thermidor, year VII (of the revolutionary calendar; 29 July 1799), four days after the victory at Abukir. It was distinguished by the presence of Sheikh El-Mahdi, the Divan's secretary; his unexpected arrival at nightfall caused a sensation. This Egyptian notable was received with respect and full honours. An interpreter translated for him the gist of the papers read.

The record of the Institute's sessions has never been found. It was probably burned in 1807 at Napoleon's command, along with other archives of the Egyptian expedition judged compromising. Nevertheless, we know that six subjects were discussed on 29 July 1799, illustrating this scientific academy's eclecticism:[1] the engineer Michel-Ange Lancret reported the discovery of the Rosetta Stone; the zoologist Étienne Geoffroy Saint-Hilaire presented a strange fish of the Nile, the tetrodon; the mathematician Gaspard Monge examined 'a curved surface all of whose normals are tangent to the same sphere'; the botanist Alire Raffeneau-Delile compared the descriptions and appellations of several Egyptian plants; the architect Charles Louis Balzac described the ruins of a large circus in Alexandria where Pompey's column was located; finally, a poet, Parseval Grandmaison, whose mediocre works annoyed the audience, declaimed an ode he had written on the victory of Abukir, the news of which had that very day reached Cairo.

Thus at the opening of the session, 'a letter was read in which Citizen Lancret, a member of the Institute, informed the audience that Citizen Bouchard, an officer of the engineering corps, had discovered inscriptions in the city of Rosetta which may prove very interesting to examine. The black stone bearing these inscriptions is divided into three horizontal bands: the lowest contains several lines of Greek characters that were inscribed under the reign of Ptolemy Philopator; the second inscription is written in unknown characters; and the third contains only hieroglyphs.'

This announcement did not seem to interest Sheikh El-Mahdi, even though he was considered one of the most brilliant luminaries of the Islamic university in Cairo. He spoke only to comment with astonishment on Geoffroy Saint-Hilaire's study on the tetrodon, exclaiming 'What! So many words for a single fish? I am truly sorry for the author if he is obliged to say as much about each of the species that live in the water ... In this vast universe the All-Powerful has created more than fifty thousand different species of fish ...'

The importance of the Rosetta Stone also escaped an observer as vigilant as Abd-al-Rahman al-Jabarti: this Cairo notable's celebrated chronicle, in which he recorded, day-by-day, in the manner of an ethnologist, what the French said and did, did not even mention the discovery of the stela.[2] For an Egyptian of the end of the eighteenth century, ancient civilization was pagan, and deserved no more than scorn. Only Europeans were interested in these stone remains, which the local people liked to use as construction material, that is if they did not turn away from them in dread ...

An article and a note

The *Courrier d'Égypte*, a newspaper published in Cairo for the French expeditionary corps, did not report the discovery made in Rosetta until 29 Fructidor (15 September, no. 37), and with a certain inaccuracy. This paper was not exactly a model of journalism; its editors even managed to misspell its own title – *Courier* with one 'r'.

Rosetta, 2 Fructidor, year VII
During the fortification work that Citizen Dhautpoul, head of the engineering battalion, has been carrying out at the former Fort Rashid, now known as Fort Julien, situated on the left bank of the Nile, three thousand *toises* [about 6,000 metres] from the mouth of the Rosetta branch of the river, a stone of fine black granite, with a very delicate grain and very hard to the hammer, has been found. It is 36 inches high, 28 inches wide and from 9 to 10 inches thick. A single, well-polished side offers three inscriptions distinct from each other and arranged in three parallel bands. The first and upper inscription, written in hieroglyphic characters, consists of 14 lines, but some have been lost because the stone is broken. The second, intermediary inscription, in characters thought to be Syrian, consists of 32 lines. The third and last inscription is written in Greek; there are 54 lines of delicate, carefully engraved characters. Like those of the two other inscriptions, they are very well preserved.

General Menou has had part of the Greek inscription translated. In substance, it says that Ptolemy Philopator had all Egypt's canals reopened, and that to this work he devoted a very considerable number of labourers, immense sums and eight years of his reign. This text is of great interest for the study of hieroglyphic characters; perhaps it will even finally provide the key to deciphering them.

Citizen Bouchard, the officer in the engineering corps who conducted the work at the fort in Rashid under the direction of Citizen Dhautpoul, has been entrusted with transporting this stone to Cairo. It is now in Bulak.

La Décade égyptienne, an excellent review that published the papers presented at the Institute, gave a more substantial report. The latter's author, Jean-Joseph Marcel, was only twenty-two years old, but he was one of the best orientalists at Napoleon's disposal, especially after dysentery carried off Venture de Paradis during the siege of Saint-Jean d'Acre.

Marcel's great-uncle had been French consul in Egypt. In the spring of 1798, the organizers of the Commission of Arts and Sciences, knowing that he was interested in oriental languages, sought him out at the Imprimerie nationale (the national press) in Paris, where he was then working. He brought his equipment with him as he crossed the Mediterranean on board *L'Orient*, the admiral's ship, and it was he who printed at sea the first proclamation – in Arabic – addressed to the Egyptians. Marcel's knowledge of Arabic and Persian was not of much help in understanding the language of the pharaohs, but at least he tried to be precise:

This stone is about three feet high, twenty-seven inches wide and six inches thick.

The hieroglyphic inscription consists of fourteen lines, whose figures, six lines in dimension [sic], are arranged from left to right.

The second inscription, which was first said to be in Syrian, and then in Coptic, is composed of thirty-two lines of characters arranged in the same way as the upper inscription; they are evidently cursive characters of the ancient Egyptian language. I have found identical forms on papyrus scrolls and on a few strips of cloth enveloping human mummies.

The Greek inscription, which consists of fifty-four lines, is remarkable above all because it contains several words,

including, for example, Ftâ (God), which are not Greek but
Egyptian, and thus indicates that it was composed during the
period when, despite the efforts of the Ptolemaic rulers, the
common language of the Egyptians began to be combined with
that of the Greeks, their conquerors. This mixture increased
and eventually, towards the fourth century BCE, formed the
ancient Coptic language of which we find precious traces in
modern Coptic.

This stone appears to have been inscribed around 157 BCE, at
the beginning of the reign of Ptolemy Philometor, and not
Philopator, the name of this latter prince, who reigned around
195 BCE, figuring alongside those of Philadelphus, Euergetes
and Epiphanes in the list of gods or deified kings who preceded
the prince whose coronation and inauguration the inscription
reports. A separate memorandum will discuss in detail this
infinitely interesting stone and the ceremonies it describes.[3]

While he was more exact than the anonymous writer in the
Courrier de l'Égypte, Marcel got the king's name wrong: it was in
fact Ptolemy V Epiphanes. The date Marcel gave was incorrect
as well: it was later shown that this decree was issued on 18
Mechir of the ninth year of the reign, that is, on 27 March 196
BCE.

Three modes of reproduction

The Rosetta Stone arrived in Bulak, Cairo's port, towards the
end of Thermidor (that is, the middle of August). Bouchard did
no more than accompany it there, having been transferred,
that same month to the fort at Al-Arish, a French outpost near
the Syrian border. There he had less luck: after part of the gar-
rison mutinied, the fort fell into the hands of the Ottomans.
Bouchard was taken prisoner and mistreated, but was freed,
and went on to take part in further battles. He left a detailed

The Rosetta Stone, as reproduced in the Description de l'Égypte.

account of the fall of Al-Arish, but unfortunately for us, not a single line about the discovery of the Rosetta Stone.

When it arrived in Bulak, 'everyone hurried to see the marvellous stone, everyone wanted to analyse it in every detail', witnesses said. No doubt their concern to emphasize this enthusiasm led them to exaggerate a bit: 'The scholars who were then in Cairo spent days, even weeks, examining it, and this close examination only confirmed the high hopes they had regarding it.'[4]

It very soon became necessary to make copies of the document. Draughtsmen set to work, but before long they realized that their work would be very time-consuming, and in any case would not be absolutely precise. The slightest imperfection could skew comparisons among the three scripts, and thus the lines of reasoning that might make it possible to decipher the hieroglyphs.

The members of the Commission of Arts and Sciences then began to compete to see who could reproduce the precious Stone most precisely. Three methods were tried in succession.

Jean-Joseph Marcel, the director of the Cairo Press, developed for this purpose a new technique, which he called 'autography', which was popularized in Europe only a decade later. The Stone was first carefully cleaned so as to remove any foreign bodies from its surface. Then it was dried by wiping it carefully in such a way that the indentions remained full of water and did not absorb the ink that was spread on the projecting surfaces. When the stela was half dried, printer's ink was spread on it, and then damp paper was pressed against it. On the impression thus formed, the letters appeared in white against a black background, as on the Stone itself, but in reverse. To restore the original appearance of the text, the paper had to be read as a transparency or in a mirror. With the assistance of Antoine Galland, a proof-reader at the Cairo Press, Marcel was able to make several printed copies in this way on 24 January 1800.

The Rosetta Stone also attracted the attention of Nicolas Conté, an ingenious man who was in charge of the mechanical workshops in Cairo and had already produced a number of technical exploits. Conté tried another mode of reproducing the text on the Stone, precisely the opposite of the one Marcel had used: tracing. This time, the Stone was used like an engraved copper plate. The surface, treated with a mixture of rubber and nitric acid, did not retain the ink, whereas the indentions, which had been filled with a greasy material, did. By pressing a sheet of paper against the Stone, Conté obtained black, clear-cut inscriptions, very well-defined, against a colourless background.

Proof sheets made using each method were given to General Dugua. In the spring of 1800, he returned to France and delivered the sheets to the National Institute in Paris.

A third technique was tried with similar success by an engineer, Adrien Raffeneau-Delile (the botanist's brother). He employed a proven method, casting, using sulphur. Years later, his work, which was very carefully executed, turned out to be of special value in preparing a reproduction of the stela for inclusion in the Commission's great collective work, the *Description de l'Égypte*.

Thus the Rosetta Stone was preserved in three different ways. It remained only to decipher it, which was quite another matter.

CHAPTER THREE

Sacred signs and symbols

I N T H E fourth century CE, after having been written and spoken for more than three thousand years, the Egyptian language disappeared in all its most traditional forms. The emperor Theodosius having prohibited the practice of pagan cults, no more hieroglyphic texts were written in the Nile valley. As the years went by, no one was any longer able to decipher this writing that was so rich in signs and engraved on stones or drawn on papyri. It soon came to be seen as having a mysterious if not magical character.

The last Egyptian priests did not leave behind a grammar that would make it possible to understand the mechanics of their language. When the Rosetta Stone was discovered in 1799, the enigma was still intact. The few clues available came from two sources: the writings of ancient Greek and Roman authors who had taken an interest in this language but not really studied it, and the pioneering efforts of a few European scholars who had, since the Renaissance, sought to decipher it in a more or less rational manner.

Greek readings, Roman readings

The Greeks and Romans, who had dominated Egypt for centuries, could hardly fail to be interested in the local language. Relatively skilful descriptions of it were written by several authors, including the fourth-century historian Ammianus Marcellinus, who explained that 'The language of the first Egyptians did not have, like modern languages, a set number of characters corresponding to all the needs of thought. The value of a noun or verb was attached to each letter, and sometimes a letter constituted a complete meaning.'[1] Ammianus gave the example of the bee, which expresses the word 'king', because, he claimed, 'if sweetness is the essence of government, the presence of a stinger still sometimes has to make itself felt' – a purely imaginary explanation, but one whose fundamental conception is none the less correct.

Herodotus emphasized that Egyptians 'have two sorts of writing, sacred and common'.[2] Diodorus Siculus, who had travelled in the Nile valley, added that 'In the education of their sons the Priests teach them two kinds of writing, that which is called "sacred", and that which is used in the more general instruction.'[3] As a sacred writing, the hieroglyphs were thus supposed to be thenceforth limited to a priestly élite, whereas a simpler cursive script for ordinary use was accessible to everyone else.

Thus confined to sacred usage, the hieroglyphs presupposed initiation. The latter was described by Apuleius, who came from North Africa and was attracted by all forms of mystical spirituality: 'After the ceremony of opening had been celebrated with the prescribed ritual and the morning sacrifice had been completed, he brought out from the secret part of the sanctuary some books inscribed with unknown characters. Some used the shapes of all sorts of animals to represent abridged expressions of liturgical language; in others, the ends of the letters were knotted and curved like wheels or interwoven like vine-tendrils to protect their meaning from the curiosity of the uninitiated.'[4]

In this way, from one author to another, the image of a graphic system with symbolic or esoteric connotations was gradually established. Even Plutarch, who was better informed than most of his compatriots, was taken in: 'The Egyptians,' he wrote, 'represent their lord and king Osiris by an eye and a sceptre, and some attribute to Osiris's name the meaning "he who has many eyes" from *os* ("many" in Egyptian) and *iri* ("eye"); they also represent the heavens, which never grow old, by an asp, and anger by a heart placed above a hearth.'[5]

It may seem astonishing that none of these great authors of antiquity was sufficiently interested in languages to learn Egyptian. It is possible that foreign visitors were rarely initiated to hieroglyphic writing by the priests of ancient Egypt. But nothing prevented them from learning the spoken language of the time and its script (demotic, widely used). Should this lack of interest be attributed to the cultural gap, or to rivalry between two modes of thought, Egyptian on one hand, and Greek and Roman on the other? In Alexandria, a city open to all currents of thought, while classical authors were studied, encyclopedias were compiled and the Bible was translated into Greek, hardly any effort was made to introduce Egyptians to Greek literature or Greeks to Egyptian science.

However, bilingualism was not unusual. Many literary papyri and school exercises in Greek, which have been found all over the Nile valley, showed the popularity then enjoyed by Greek poetry, prose and theatre. Conversely, many Greek intellectuals came to Egypt to study Egyptian theology and medicine.

Egyptomaniac fantasies

In the third century, Coptic appeared, and quickly supplanted demotic, becoming the official language of the Alexandrian Church. This language retained the grammar used since the New Empire, as well as the traditional pronunciation and vocabulary, but was written in Greek letters complemented by a few demotic signs. All this no longer had anything to do with the texts inscribed on the walls of the temples.

When Arabic was definitively established in Egypt, towards the end of the first millenium CE, Coptic ceased to be a living language and was thereafter used only in the Christian liturgy. But Egyptian texts, in a more or less degenerate form, continued to be translated or to inspire various works that were read in the new intellectual centres of late antiquity and the early Middle Ages, such as Byzantium, Baghdad, Damascus, Esfahan and Samarkand.

During the Middle Ages and the Renaissance, the myth of Isis played a privileged role in Western culture. The interest in the cult of Isis, and in the Neo-Platonists and hermetism in general, made Egypt fashionable. People began again to read Apuleius's and Ovid's *Metamorphoses*, and Plutarch's 'Isis and Osiris'. Works inspired by them were composed by great authors such as Boccaccio and by many others whose writings have not come down to us.

A Greek translation of hieroglyphic inscriptions on an Egyptian obelisk in Rome was discovered in a German monastery in 1414. This incomplete text, thought to have been originally written by a certain Hermapion, was brought to Florence. It led to the first efforts to decipher the hieroglyphs and fascinated generations of researchers.

In 1419, Cristoforo Bundelmonti, a traveller and archaeologist, found on the Greek island of Andros a copy of Horapollon's *Hieroglyphica*. Initially circulated in manuscript in Florence, and published in Venice shortly after the invention of printing, this text was frequently reproduced and translated throughout the Renaissance. Dealing, sign by sign, only with the allegorical aspect of the hieroglyphs, the author offered an image of them that largely coincided with medieval bestiaries and Christian symbols representing the components of nature. This work became authoritative and inspired a number of others.

Around 1439, Cosimo de' Medici founded the Platonic

Academy in Florence that served as the framework for an artistic, literary, philosophical and scientific movement that sought to reproduce the intellectual climate of third-century Alexandria. Thinkers and artists tried to reconcile Christian dogma with Neo-Platonic philosophy, as was shown for example by the figure of 'Hermes Trismegistos, a contemporary of Moses' among the prophets represented on the floor of the cathedral in Siena. The hieroglyphs, the key to Egyptian culture, were amalgamated with an esotericism that became increasingly influential.

Only a short step separated studying, admiring and imitating the ancients from counterfeiting them. The Dominican Giovanni Nanni wrote a dozen apocryphal texts, attributed to classical authors, which sought to demonstrate that Egypt had directly influenced Italy. He created a 'heroic' genealogy for the Borgias by making them descendants of the Egyptian Hercules, the son of Osiris. In the Vatican, on the ceiling of the *Sala dei Santi*, Pinturicchio painted between 1492 and 1495 frescoes representing episodes from the myth of Isis and Osiris and the triumph of the Apis bull, in which the prototype of the family's heraldic bull was seen.

In 1525 the Mensa Isiaca, considered one of the most important ancient monuments, was discovered in Rome. Countless strange theories regarding it were immediately elaborated. Other monuments related to Isis were found in Rome's Villa Adriana. And while Egyptian obelisks were being exhumed in order to set them up in squares in the Holy City, creative works influenced by Egyptian art were being produced all over Europe. Egyptomania was in full swing, accompanied by irrational or simply fantastic acts.

Athanasius Kircher discovers Coptic

At the same time, amid the sulphureous vapours emerging

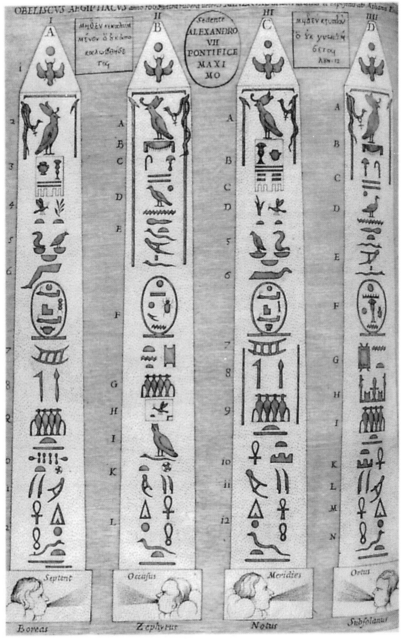

The four faces of the obelisk in the Piazza della Minerva in Rome, copied with relatively few errors by Athanasius Kircher (Obelisci Aegyptiaci, Rome, 1666, plate facing p. 13).

from the alchemists' laboratories, the first steps towards a scientific approach to the problem were taken. Interest in philology was developing in the great cities of Europe, to the point that languages and scripts were being compared that had nothing to do with each other. Coptic was rediscovered, although it was still losing ground in Egypt. In 1626 Pietro della Valle, a Roman traveller, brought a large number of manuscripts back from the Near East, including five grammars and two Coptic–Arabic dictionaries. These served as the basis for Athanasius Kircher's work, which was long to dominate study of the hieroglyphs.

Kircher, a German Jesuit, was the first to make a serious attempt to decipher the writing of the ancient Egyptians. He became interested in the problem in 1628, when he saw the hieroglyphic inscriptions of obelisks in Rome. Appointed to the chair of mathematics in the Roman College, Kircher was entrusted with Pietro della Valle's manuscripts. His *Prodomus coptus sive aegyptiacus*, published in 1636, is an introduction to the study of Coptic and ancient Egyptian. But it was in his *Lingua aegyptiaca restitua* (1644) that he made the best use of the documents available to him and thus laid the foundation for Coptic studies.

Kircher developed his theories further in a series of works in which he associated, for example, mummification and metempsychosis. Although his work was based on authentic documents, he returned to an esoteric view of Egyptian thought and hieroglyphic script. In ancient Egypt he saw the source of all the sciences and all philosophies. According to him, this knowledge was perceptible to the human mind only through a subtle play of symbols. Thus he interpreted each hieroglyph as the basis of a philosophical concept.

A vastly learned mystic, Athanasius Kircher sought to reconcile the multiple, contradictory aspects of universal knowledge in a sort of cosmic harmony. He was not only a mathematician and a humanist fascinated by Egyptian culture;

he combined scientific learning with an imperious need to reflect on the essence and manifestations of everything he encountered. For example, he considered optics to be a science, but focused his attention on the metaphysical interpretations to which it gave rise and the illusions that resulted from them ... He invented the magic lantern.

As curator of the Roman College's collections, Kircher was able to acquire all sorts of antiquities, in particular Egyptian ones. His works reproduced a large number of monuments and hieroglyphic inscriptions brought back by travellers. Although he went completely wrong in his attempt to decipher the hieroglyphics, and although he maintained indefensible theories, such as the Greek origin of Coptic, we owe him the crucial assertion that Coptic is the surviving form of the common language of the ancient Egyptians.

A few glimmers

Several great thinkers of the seventeenth and eighteenth centuries took an interest in the enigma of the hieroglyphics. Leibniz, who was a philosopher and a theologian before becoming a mathematician, admired Kircher, but did not accept his views regarding the identity of Coptic and Egyptian. He was inclined to believe that the language of the pharaohs was Armenian in origin. The inscriptions on the obelisks inspired in him more rational reflections, since he was the first to assert that they contained 'historical texts commemorating events and victories'. Newton also left his preferred areas of endeavour – mathematics, physics and astronomy – to write a historical study[6] far less admired than his scientific works.

In the eighteenth century, archaeology was in vogue, and it was fashionable to publish learned correspondence. The *Recueil d'antiquités égyptiennes, étrusques, grecques, romaines et gauloises*, by Baron Caylus, appeared in eight volumes, from

1752 to 1764. At the same time, travellers to Egypt composed increasingly precise and detailed narratives and descriptions of the monuments there, such as the *Description de l'Égypte* by the French Consul General, Benoît de Maillet, the Danish sailor Frederik Norden's *Travels*, the *Description of the East, and Some Other Countries*, by the Englishman Richard Pococke, and the *Reisenbeschreibung nach Arabien* by the German geographer Karsten Niebuhr.

It was in this context that the Anglican bishop of Gloucester, William Warburton, wrote his *Divine Legation of Moses*.[7] In this work he refuted the view that Egyptian script was esoteric and the 'general error' that consisted in believing that priests invented hieroglyphs in order to conceal their knowledge from the common people. This sounded like Kircher. Warburton credited the Egyptians with inventing the alphabet. According to him, they made the transition from an ideographic script to a phonetic one.

Another step forward was taken at about the same time by the man who had just deciphered the Palmyrian and Phoenician alphabets. In 1761, the Abbe Barthélemy, curator of the Cabinet royal des médailles in Paris, suggested that the ovals – or 'cartouches' – found in Egyptian inscriptions contained the names of gods or kings. This idea was taken up in 1785 by Charles Joseph de Guignes, professor of Syriac at the Collège de France and a sinologist who defended extremely debatable theories, such as that Egyptian was derived from Chinese. However, his work led him to make an important point: the Egyptians did not transcribe certain vowels. He also suspected that their three systems of writing (hieroglyphic, hieratic and demotic) composed a whole.

The Dane Jörgen Zoëga collected all the information he could find about the obelisks and other Egyptian monuments. This massive documentation led him to suggest, in 1797, that Egyptian script must include phonetic elements.[8] This offered a promising new line of approach.

Thus when the Rosetta Stone was discovered at the end of the eighteenth century, four points had already been asserted, if not established:

1   Coptic derived from the ancient language of Egypt;
2   the three Egyptian scripts (hieroglyphic, hieratic and demotic) were connected;
3   the cartouches contained royal names;
4   the system of hieroglyphs included phonetic elements.

These points were not negligible; indeed, they were crucial. But were they enough to decipher 'the stone with three inscriptions'?

CHAPTER FOUR

With the point of a compass

N APOLEON DEPARTED from Egypt on 23 August 1799, leaving behind him the Army of the East and most of the scientists and artists. He took with him the Turkish flags taken at Abukir, but not the Rosetta Stone, which had been discovered a month earlier. He merely mentioned it at the National Institute while reporting a few weeks later on the scientific and technical work carried out in the Nile valley.

Being fairly well acquainted with the history of Egypt, thanks to their study of the Greek authors of antiquity, Napoleon's scholars were able to understand why a decree dating from the second century BCE had to be bilingual, and even include three scripts. The hieroglyph, which was sacred, had to be used for a text inscribed in temples, even if in the Ptolemaic period it was already a rigid, almost dead language. The cursive script was the one in everyday use. And Greek was necessary because those who held power knew very little Egyptian.

The proof sheets taken from the Rosetta Stone were circulated among the members of the Commission of Arts and Sciences in Cairo. Everyone – engineers, architects and musicians – wondered how to move from the Greek text to one of the Egyptian scripts.

Jean-Joseph Marcel, the author of the article published in *La Décade égyptienne*, and another young orientalist, Louis Rémi Raige, were asked to look into this question. They focused their attention not on the hieroglyphic inscription, which had been badly damaged – only part of its fourteen lines had been preserved – but on the second, much more complete, inscription.

How could one read and interpret a text when neither its language nor its script was known? Marcel later put it this way: 'Had the language been known, we could have started from the Greek translation, looking for the known words that the latter's meaning provided, and by analysing their deciphering, deduce the alphabetic elements. Had the script been known but not the language, the operation would have been still easier; reading it would have yielded some words, whose interpretive value could have been sought either in modern Coptic or the contemporary version of some other ancient idiom. But in this case we were proceeding between two unknowns.'[1]

Where to begin? Marcel and Raige noted that the Greek text included numerous proper names. To find them in the Egyptian text, they made use of mathematics. The Greek inscription consisted of 54 lines, while the Egyptian inscription consisted of only 32. Using a compass, the two Frenchmen divided the two texts into correlative and proportional segments, thus establishing corresponding parts in the proportion 54 to 32. This assumed, of course, that each part of the Greek and Egyptian texts was a literal translation of the other, which was far from certain.

'Without being daunted by this concern, we moved ahead, and our success proved that our system was right,'[2] Marcel wrote years later. The two young orientalists first selected the name 'Ptolemy', which appeared eleven times in the Greek text, in lines 3, 6, 8, 9, 37, 41 and 49. By using the compass to determine the points in the Egyptian inscription corresponding to those where the name was located in the Greek inscription, they found a set of signs that were identical in each of these different places. Marcel and Raige then set out to analyse the graphic elements, thinking that in this way they could reconstitute the Egyptian alphabet.

Boldly pursuing this approach, they began by studying the 'P' in 'Ptolemy'. The corresponding figure seemed to occur in the name of Pyrra, which appeared in the fifth line of the Greek text. The 'T' that followed it was also present in the name of Aetos (in the fourth line of the Greek text). Beginning from the assumption that when writing, oriental peoples often left out small vowels, Marcel and Raige moved on to the letters 'L' and 'M', seeking comparisons with the names of Alexander and Alexandria. But they soon ran into a brick wall.

Until his death in 1810, nine years after the end of the Egyptian expedition, Louis Rémi Raige continued to examine the Rosetta Stone, hoping desperately to discover its secret. Jean-Joseph Marcel quickly returned to his studies of Arabic and Persian, leaving it to others to solve the Rosetta Stone's immense enigma. He translated fables, drew up bilingual dictionaries, and even discovered an Arabic character unknown to European orientalists, which was to be called 'rectangular kufic'.

More than one member of the Commission of Arts and Sciences was convinced that the ancient Egyptian language was indecipherable. After a lengthy examination of the texts inscribed on the ruins at El-Kab, north of Edfu, Alexandre Saint-Genis, an engineer, wrote: 'There seems to be no consistent relationship between the characters and the subjects represented, and this deprives us more than ever of the hope once entertained that it might be possible to find the key to the hieroglyphs and the cursive writing of the Egyptians.'[3]

However, it was this hope that led Napoleon's scientists, while on an exploratory mission in Upper Egypt from August to November 1799, to copy down as carefully as possible 'more than one hundred tablets with their hieroglyphs, ten new obelisks, several monoliths, basins and sarcophagi covered with hieroglyphic writing, a large number of scarabs and ancient objects bearing sacred characters, and a collection of legends and phrases found in temples and palaces', as the

Description de l'Égypte reported. They also collected 'four or five large manuscripts [...] composed of sixty-one pages of Egyptian in common script and five or six hundred columns in hieroglyphic script'.

Two other stelae

Scientists and artists were looking for bilingual documents that resembled the Rosetta Stone. Wouldn't the decree honouring Ptolemy V Epiphanes be found in all of Egypt's temples?

In autumn 1799, two young men from the École polytechnique, Jean-Marie Dubois-Aymé and Prosper Jollois, visited the little town of Minuf in the Nile delta. In front of a house, they found a rectangular stela in black granite, which was being used as a bench. It measured 0.36 metres in height and 1.20 metres in length, and on one of its faces were the remains of two inscriptions, one in Greek and the other in Egyptian cursive characters. Only the first words of the Greek text ('Of the young king, always') could be read clearly. 'The two inscriptions are in very poor condition,' Dubois-Aymé and Jollois noted. 'We have copied the first words of the first one; and the comparison we have made with the intermediate inscription on the Rosetta Stone leaves no doubt as to the identity of the letters.' Everything suggested that the stone from Minuf also had a third inscription in hieroglyphic characters.

At the end of September 1800, Philippe Caristie, an engineer working for the office of Ponts et Chaussées, discovered a black granite stone being used as a doorsill in a mosque in the Nasriya quarter of Cairo. Three texts were inscribed on it in hieroglyphs, in cursive script and in Greek. This stela was larger than the Rosetta Stone. Its characters had been largely worn away, and were almost illegible. None the less, it was possible to determine that it dated from the Ptolemaic period. On its upper part an outspread wing had been sculpted, like the ones on the globes found on the frontispieces of temples. The stela was removed from the mosque and taken to the palace of Hassan Kashef, where the meetings of the Institut d'Égypte were held.

Considering their condition, the stones discovered in Minuf and in Cairo were of far less interest than the Rosetta Stone. The latter remained a jewel. But a sterile jewel, which had not yet made it possible to make even the slightest progress towards deciphering the hieroglyphs.

CHAPTER FIVE

The spoils of war

JANUARY 1800. The atmosphere in Cairo was feverish; the Egyptian adventure begun a year and a half earlier was approaching its end. Kléber, who had taken over for Napoleon, concluded a peace treaty with the English and the Ottomans that set the terms for the French withdrawal. The scientists and artists, who were homesick, hastened to pack their trunks to leave on a number of boats. In addition to their papers and their collections, they took with them the Rosetta Stone.

Having been delayed by an epidemic of plague that forced them to hole up for more than a month on an island in the Nile, the travellers finally reached Alexandria, where other members of the Commission of Arts and Sciences joined them. But no sooner had they embarked for France upon the brig *L'Oiseau* than they heard the bad news: the peace treaty had been denounced. Kléber ordered his troops to renew combat. The scientists and artists had to wait to go home. After a month on board in the port of Alexandria, on 27 April they returned to dry land.

Was the Rosetta Stone then returned to Cairo? It seems instead that it was stored in Alexandria, though information about this is scarce and contradictory. However, nothing more was said about the stela until the military defeat of the French the following spring.

Article 16

On 18 March 1801, an English army landed near Abukir. It was followed three weeks later by a Turkish army, which arrived at Al-Arish. This time the French had to retreat, evacuating part of the delta.

Near Rosetta, Fort Julien was besieged by the British forces. The commander of the engineers in this citadel was no other than Captain Bouchard, who had returned to service on the site of his discovery. The resistance lasted six days. The two hundred French, exhausted, surrendered on 19 April. Bouchard himself related these dark days in a text preserved in the archives of the French army.[1] It consisted of a few sheets of blue paper, with letters sloping to the right, very carefully formed, with downstrokes and upstrokes. Many details, but not a single allusion to the Rosetta Stone ... The captain – excessively modest or unaware of his merits – was taken prisoner for the second time before finally returning to France the following July. He continued to have bad luck – a failed colonial expedition to Santo Domingo, hard battles in Spain and Portugal, personal difficulties after the fall of the Empire. By a final irony of fate, he died just a month and a half before the hieroglyphs were deciphered, at the age of fifty-one, on 5 August 1822.[2]

The English troops arrived at the gates of Cairo, where a new plague epidemic was ravaging the city. Confined to the citadel, the artists and scientists were divided. Some of them – including Nicolas Conté and Jean-Joseph Marcel – decided to stay where they were. The others chose to leave for Alexandria, hoping thereby to get out of Egypt more easily. A bad mistake, which was to cost them dearly ...

The first group benefited from the conditions on which the capital was surrendered: on 14 July 1801, soldiers, scientists and artists left with their arms and baggage. Thus Kléber's remains were exhumed and returned to France, while the Rosetta Stone remained in Alexandria. In the latter city, General Menou, the commander-in-chief of the Army of the East, refused to surrender, in contrast to his subordinate in Cairo, General Belliard. And it was against his will that about fifty scientists and artists embarked on board *L'Oiseau* – the same ship that was to take them home a year earlier – but had to leave their collections behind. Their sea voyage lasted several weeks, and ended ... in Alexandria, the British admiral having prevented them from passing.

Menou was forced to recognize his defeat by the English and the Ottomans on 26 August, and he asked for an armistice. A draft surrender agreement, drawn up by the French generals, was submitted to the leaders of the English army. Article 16 stipulated that 'The individuals composing the Institute of Egypt and the Commission of arts, shall carry with them all the papers, plans, memoirs, collections of natural history, and all the monuments of art and antiquity collected by them in Egypt'. Obviously, the Rosetta Stone figured among the most prominent of these objects.

Lieutenant-General Sir John Hely Hutchinson, commander-in-chief of the British army, rejected Article 16, on the advice of a young scholar, William Richard Hamilton, secretary to the English ambassador in Constantinople, who had been sent to him on special assignment. The response was: 'The members of the Institute may carry with them all the instruments of arts and science, which they have brought from France; but the Arabian manuscripts, the statues, and other collections which have been made for the French Republic, shall be considered as public property, and subject to the disposal of the generals of the combined army.'

An epistolary duel

The scientists having protested strongly, Menou promised that he would have Article 16 modified and he wrote to Hutchinson to this effect. The two men exchanged several letters. On 14 Fructidor, year IX (1 September 1801), the French general assured his English counterpart that 'I declare here, in the name of honour, Monsieur le Général, that as regards collections, none of the small number that exist here belongs to the French Republic; all of them were made at the expense and through the efforts of individuals. I know of no other objects that could be considered property of the Republic apart from two sarcophagi, one taken in Alexandria, and the other from Cairo ...'[3]

This was a great lie. Hadn't Menou written to Joseph Fourier, secretary of the Institut d'Égypte, on the preceding 21 May: 'As for the material collections of antiquities, mineralogy, etc., it is clear that they belong to the government and that they must be deposited'?[4] In fact, the scientists and artists had not been allowed to board L'Oiseau until they had left behind these objects considered to be public property.

The English were not taken in when Menou claimed that the Rosetta Stone was his personal property. Later on, one of them commented that 'General Menou maintained that two statues found in the ruins of Alexandria were private property, belonging to General Friant; that the famous stone (called the gem of antiquity by the French, as being the key to the hieroglyphic language), was his private property, and that the collections of natural history belonged individually to the different artists. These pretensions were so weak as not to admit of sound arguments; for how could such things be claimed by individuals, particularly in the French service, on an expedition, in which so much attention had been paid, and so much national expense incurred, to procure for the museum of Paris curiosities of this nature?'[5]

General Hutchinson's patience was exhausted. On 5 September he curtly informed Menou that 'When I demand the Arabic manuscripts, statues, and several collections and antique objects, I am only following the fine example you set for Europe. Were you at war with the Belvedere Apollo, the Laocöon and several of the fine things you took from Rome? [...] In all the countries where the French have waged war, they have seized everything that seemed to them suitable to take. Since the fate of arms has decided against you, I demand the execution of the surrender on this point. [...] I demand all these objects and you may be sure that I shall not let a single part of them leave for France.'[6]

Menou was furious, and in a letter dated the following day he wrote to Hutchinson: 'The English have long set an example for the whole universe, Monsieur le Général, by taking whatever suited them [...] . No doubt you have the right of the stronger, and you exercise it as you wish ...' And further on: 'It is true, Monsieur le Général, that I have in my possession a stone that I had unearthed in Rosetta and that bears three different inscriptions. It was my property, but I declare to you that I truly intended to give it to the Republic upon my return to France. You want it, Monsieur le Général, and you shall have it because you are the stronger and I will not be sorry to let it be known in Europe that my property has been taken from me at the command of Monsieur the English general.'[7]

Outraged, on 12 September Hutchinson attempted to put an end to this epistolary duel: 'You are trying to deprive me of everything you can. You have claimed that the stone found in Rosetta is your own property and that the two statues unearthed in Alexandria belong to General Friant. You are well aware, General, that these objects have always been considered as belonging to the French Republic, all Egypt and your whole army know that as well as I do [...]. I have said ten times, and I repeat, that I want all these objects ...'

Menou's reply, written on 13 September, adopted a grandiloquent tone: 'If I were to order that anything but public property be handed over to you, I should so far transgress the limits of justice, my duties and the authority entrusted in me that I would deserve to lose my head.' He added: 'Only when I am in Europe, Monsieur le Général, shall I mention again the stone, my property, which you are so good as to take from me.'

The scientists' threat

Seeing that Menou had no standing with the English, and in any case had no means of making them yield on this point, two scientists, the botanist Delile and the zoologist Savigny, notified him in the name of their colleagues that they were prepared to accompany their collections to London and to make their case to the English government. Menou, beside himself, then added this postscript to Hutchinson: 'I have just learned that several of our collectors want to follow their seeds, minerals, birds, butterflies or reptiles wherever you send their boxes. I don't know if they will have themselves stuffed for it, but I can assure you that if they take it into their heads to do so, I will not stand in their way. I have allowed them to address themselves to you.'

Delile, Savigny and the zoologist Geoffroy Saint-Hilaire were sent as delegates to the English general. They addressed him in these terms: 'You are depriving us of our collections, our drawings, our maps, our copies of hieroglyphs; but who will give you the key to all this? They are mere sketches, which must be complemented by our personal impressions, our observations and our memories. Without us, these materials are a dead language you will not understand at all, neither you nor your scientists.'[8] And they made this threat: 'Rather than let this iniquitous and barbarous despoliation occur, we will scatter everything in the middle of the Libyan sands or throw it into the sea; then we will publicly protest in Europe, and tell what violence has forced us to destroy so many treasures.'

General Hutchinson, who listened coldly to their plea, told them that his reply would be brought to them by Hamilton. The same day, Hamilton presented himself before the French scientists: the answer was no. Then Geoffroy Saint-Hilaire exploded: 'No, no, we shall not obey. It will be two days before your army enters here. Well, then! By that time the sacrifice will have been completed. Then you can do with us as you will. No, I tell you, it shall not be said that such a sacrifice could take place. We shall burn our riches ourselves. You want fame. Well, you can count on history remembering this: you too shall have burned a library in Alexandria.'[9]

Shaken by so much determination, Hamilton promised to find a solution. This cultivated young man, who was soon after to translate the Greek text on the Rosetta Stone himself,[10] pleaded the case of those whom he wished to despoil ... The British finally met the French half-way, letting the scientists retain their notes, drawings and natural history collections, but keeping the most important antiquities.

The Rosetta Stone was stored in General Menou's residence, in a wooden case, wrapped in cotton fabric and protected by a double mat. Accompanied by a detachment of artillerymen, Colonel Turner, commander of the third regiment of guards, took possession of it one afternoon. He had the Stone transported to his own residence, 'through narrow streets, subjected to the sarcasm of many French officers and soldiers'.[11] Later he authorized certain members of the Commission of Arts and Sciences to make a new reproduction of it, 'on the condition that the stone should not suffer any damage'.

Seventeen 'ancient sculptures, taken from the French army in Alexandria' were listed in the inventory made by Colonel Turner and countersigned by Joseph Fourier, the secretary of the Institut d'Égypte. Among them was the sarcophagus found in a mosque in the city, the wrist of a colossus from Memphis and a black granite statue from Abydos. The most desired piece was listed eighth: 'a stone of black granite, with three inscriptions, in hieroglyphs, Coptic and Greek, found near Rosetta'. In Coptic ... Obviously this second script remained controversial.

Menou thus lost his battle. That did not prevent him from writing with admirable sang-froid, on the following 21 November, to Chaptal, the French Minister of the Interior, to inform him that he had succeeded in saving 'the various collections' made by the scientists 'after a long struggle' with the ·English general. 'The monuments that can be considered public,' he added, 'remained in the hands of the English, but I shall forcefully demand the return of a stone covered with inscriptions that was found in Rosetta, when I was commander there. I had declared it to be my own property, and I assure you, Citoyen Ministre, that this property in truth belonged to the Republic. I dare to hope that you, as a friend of the arts, will use all your influence to see to it that this precious monument is not lost to France.'[12]

The objects seized were put on board two boats for shipment to England. The Rosetta Stone, however, did not leave Egypt until a few months later, on the frigate *L'Égyptienne*, escorted by Colonel Turner, who was ultimately to be promoted to the rank of general. This time, it was not a false departure: the 'stone with three inscriptions' was never to return to the valley of the Nile.

CHAPTER SIX

King George's gift

W HEN IT arrived in Portsmouth in February 1802, the Rosetta Stone was not immediately placed in the British Museum. Orientalists were able to arrange to study it for several months at the Society of Antiquaries in London. In April, one of the members of this venerable institution, the Reverend Stephen Weston, presented an English translation of the Greek text, together with some commentaries. In July, the Society had plaster casts made of the Stone, which were sent to four universities (Cambridge, Dublin, Edinburgh and Oxford), and facsimiles of the text were dispatched to various institutions in Europe and America: the Vatican, the Imperial Library in Vienna, the Berlin Academy, the National Institute and the National Library in Paris, the Royal Antiquities Society in Copenhagen, the University of Leiden, the Philosophical Society in Philadelphia, and so on. Each of these was asked to provide a translation and comments on the Greek text.[1]

There was no reply. Did the stela's poor condition and incompleteness discourage scholars? Since no help had been received, at the meeting on 4 November the Reverend Weston himself presented an English translation of what seemed to be the whole of the Greek text. However, a week later the Society of Antiquaries received a Latin translation, with numerous comments in French made by Professor C. G. Heyne of the University of Göttingen in Germany.

Understandably enough, orientalists and Hellenists

focused on the only script with which they were familiar – Greek. On 2 December, for instance, a member of the Society of Antiquaries, Taylor Combe, argued that the decree could not have been published during the lifetime of Ptolemy Epiphanes. Several other specialists discussed words or parts of words that had disappeared from the stela. One of these contributions – Professor Porson's – was used as the basis for future facsimiles.

At the end of 1802, the Rosetta Stone was officially presented to the British Museum as a gift from King George III. The British Museum, which had been established half a century earlier at the instigation of a wealthy collector, Sir Hans Sloane, still had only a small Egyptian collection. The seventeen pieces seized in Alexandria gave it new lustre. The Rosetta Stone in particular attracted scholars and pilgrims.[2] On one side of the stela was written in white paint: 'Captured in Egypt by the British Army in 1801'. And on the other side: 'Presented by King George III'.

Citizen Ameilhon's study

The scientists in Paris had a head start on their English colleagues, for since 1800 two impressions of the stela had been available to them. These documents, which had been brought from Egypt by General Dugua, were presented to the National Institute, and the Hellenist Laporte-Dutheil, a member of the department of literature and fine arts, was asked to examine them. But being forced to leave Paris, he quickly abandoned the project, which was completed by one of his colleagues, 'Citizen Ameilhon', of the department of ancient history and literature.

Ameilhon, a linguist, presented his colleagues with a study of the Greek inscription during the session on 15 Nivôse, year IX (6 January 1801). He was encouraged to publish this work, but he preferred to wait for the stela to arrive in Paris so that he could examine it more closely. While the Greek inscription may 'make it easier to understand those in Coptic or Egyptian', he explained, 'the latter might in turn throw some light on some obscure parts of the former, and even provide me with the materials to fill in the gaps that mar the text's coherence'. A remarkable expression of optimism, or perhaps of presumption ...

The announcement of the French defeat and the transportation of the stela to London made Ameilhon change his mind. 'Now that we have lost the Rosetta Stone,' he wrote in May 1803, 'I have made up my mind to publish this work.'[3]

Oddly, the impressions that were made in London and sent to the National Institute do not correspond to those made in Egypt by Napoleon's scientists. 'I am astonished,' Ameilhon wrote, 'that these two letters "P" and "N" are so well-shaped in the English facsimile, whereas they are so imperfectly shaped in our copy. Might it be that the engraver they employed made some improvements of his own, and in a few cases allowed himself to give too fine a shape to characters that were only partly formed on the stone? Why, for example, should all the omicrons, thetas and omegas have a polygonal [sic] form in the English facsimile, whereas in General Dugua's copy none of these characters is rounded?'

Like a good Frenchman, Citizen Ameilhon had confidence in the impressions made by his compatriots, Marcel's, Conté's and Raffeneau-Delile's seeming to him 'in perfect conformity in every respect'. He gave a version of the Greek inscription printed in cursive letters, without adding any punctuation, so as to 'allow the reader complete liberty and not to prejudice his judgement'. But he warned the reader that in this text, several letters might be confused with each other: 'Often, the alpha and the lambda resemble each other so closely that no difference between them can be discerned; one can say almost the same about the theta and the omicron ... Sometimes the sigma looks like the *epsilon*, and the *mu* like the *nu*. Finally, there are many letters which, viewed separately, appear to be only partially formed ...'

Alongside the Greek inscription Ameilhon provided a 'very literal' Latin translation that made no pretensions to elegance of style. Then he offered a 'less slavish' French translation, in which the gaps in the Greek text were filled in more boldly, even if sometimes they were no more than 'simple conjectures'.

Ameilhon's French version was considered authoritative for more than four decades, until Jean-Antoine Letronne published his translation (1841), which revealed a number of defects in Ameilhon's. The first German translation, by W. Drumann, appeared in 1822, and the first Italian translation, by Ricardi, in 1833. There was no lack of English translations: Plumptre (1802), Duane (1803), and later on, Birch (1825) and Bean (1827). There was also a Latin text prepared by Bailey (1816) in addition to those produced by Ameilhon and Heyne.

The curiosity of Hellenists and historians regarding the Greek inscription on the Rosetta Stone is comprehensible. 'This text, taken by itself and independent of the interest of comparing it with the two others, offers us an extremely intriguing historical document,' Letronne wrote. 'The decree that it preserves for us, issued in honour of Ptolemy Ephiphanes by the priests of Egypt assembled in Memphis for his coronation ceremony, is so far unique; and it is also the main source that may shed some light on the fusion which, following Alexander's conquest of Egypt, combined the civil and religious customs of the two peoples.'[4]

Ameilhon himself asserted, with a certain self-satisfaction, that the Greek inscription on the stela might have allowed him to write a voluminous work 'on Egyptian chronology, geography, the history of each of the princes and princesses whose names appear in the inscription, the hierarchy of the various kinds of priests, Egyptian divinities, sacred animals, ceremonial, the form of temples and countless other subjects that might have provided ample material for the pen of a man of letters who wanted to parade his erudition'.

The decree issued in Memphis was the first of its kind to be scrutinized by Hellenists. Though written in Egypt in honour of Ptolemaic sovereigns, it falls within the domain of specialists in Greek. Only much later would it be possible to compare it with Egyptian decrees and to distinguish what belonged to each of the two cultures.

None the less, even taken in isolation, this long text included an incredible amount of information concerning the policies of the Ptolemaic rulers and the cult of which they were the object. Although Napoleon's scientists noted in particular the restoration and maintenance of Egypt's canals, many other subjects were also mentioned: donations and regular incomes accorded to the temples, fiscal privileges, exemption from taxes and obligatory work duty, amnesties for prisoners, military measures and respect for the gods, their sacred animals and their rites.

In short, the Ptolemaic rulers conducted themselves as genuine pharaohs. Accordingly, the priests who had gathered in Memphis established for Ptolemy V Ephiphanes, on the occasion of the eighth anniversary of his coronation, a statuary cult. This cult, which consisted in placing an effigy of the king in every sanctuary in Egypt, facing the local god, was part of the most classical tradition of the Egyptian monarchy, even if the form it took came from the Hellenic world.

The Greek inscription of the Memphis Decree continued to be examined by Hellenists and historians for decades. However, at the moment, what was intriguing and fascinating about the Rosetta Stone were the two other inscriptions, those in hieroglyphics and in demotic, which only a few charlatans claimed to have deciphered.

CHAPTER SEVEN

Description, for want of something better

T HE ROSETTA STONE was naturally accorded a
prominent place in the *Description de l'Égypte*, a monumental work in twenty-three volumes that was supposed to contain
all the observations made by Napoleon's scientists. When it
was published, an extra five hundred copies of the plate representing the stela were printed separately.[1]

The cast made in Cairo by Raffeneau-Delile was used to
reproduce the Greek and demotic inscriptions.[2] The hieroglyphic text was drawn twice, using Raffeneau's sulphur cast
and the plaster impression made in London.[3] One of the men
in charge of producing the *Description*, Edme François Jomard,
went to London in late 1814 in order to make impressions of
the Rosetta Stone and several other monuments. He was very
civilly received by Sir Joseph Banks, who had accompanied
Captain Cook on his voyages, and was able to carry out his
mission.[4] A note of thanks published in the *Description* did not
spare the adjectives: 'It is to the enlightened zeal of Sir Joseph
Banks and to his love for the sciences that we owe our possession of a plaster cast of the monument, and we owe no less to
Mr Taylor Combe, the curator of antiquities in the British
Museum, for the good will and attentiveness with which he
provided the author of the drawing with everything he needed

FRANÇAIS.	HÉBREU.	ARABE.	INITIALES.	MÉDIALES.	FINALES.
A.	א	ا	١ , ﻌ	١	١ .
B.	ב	ﻴ	. . .	٣ ﻟ . ٤ ﻟ	. . . .
G.	ג	ﺟ	. . .	. . . .	. . . .
D.	ד	د	. . .	٥ ٦	٧ ٢
H.	ה	ﻫ	. . .	٧)١	٨ ‖)١
O, ou.	ו	و	٩	١٠ ١١	١٢ ١٣
Z.	ז	ز	. . .	. . . . .	. . . .
Hh.	ח	ح	. . .	١٤ ١٥ ١٦	١٧ ١٨
Tt.	ט	ط	. . .	١٩	. . . .
I, y.	י	ى	٢٠	٢١ ٢٢ . ٢٣ /// ٢٤ ⫴ ٢٥	٢٦ ٢٧ ٢٨
K.	כ	ك	. . .	٢٩	. . . .
L.	ל	ل	. . .	٣٠ ٣١ (ll.)	٣٢
M.	מ	م	٣٣ ٣٤	٣٥ ٣٦	٣٧
N.	נ	ن	. . .	٣٨	٣٩
S.	ס	ش	. . .	٤٠	. . . .
A', E'.	ע	ع	٤١	. . . .	. . . .
P, ph, f.	פ	ف	٤٢ ٤٣	٢	٤٤
Ss.	צ	ص	. . .	٤٥ ٤٦ ٤٧	. . . .
Q.	ק	ق	. . .	. . . .	. . . .
R.	ר	ر	٤٨	٤٩ douteux.	٥٠
Ch.	ש	ش	٥١ ٥٢	٥٣ ٥٤	٥٥
T.	ת	ت	٥٦	٥٧ ٥٨ ٥٩	. . . .
Dd.	ץ	ظ	. . .	douteux.	. . . .
Kh.	ח	خ	. . .	٦٠	. . . .
X.	. . .	. . .	. . .	٦١	. . . .

Rémi Raige's attempt at a comparative alphabet, reproduced in the Description de l'Égypte.

to make this valuable impression.'⁵ The battle in Alexandria and the acerbic letters exchanged by General Menou and General Hutchinson seem to have been forgotten.

In the *Description* – a triumph of publishing at the beginning of the nineteenth century, for which a paper, a format and an engraving machine had been specially invented – the smallest details of the Rosetta Stone were reproduced 'with religious care'. Its 'broken and worn parts' had to be shown as faithfully as possible.

Since they could not decipher the two Egyptian inscriptions, the authors of the *Description* limited themselves to describing the stela as precisely as they could. 'The stone is black granite: its average thickness is 0.27 metres (10 inches), the width of its lower part 0.735 metres (2ds 3° 2′), and its height, in its present state, 0.963 metres (2ds 11° 7′), for unfortunately the upper part has been greatly truncated, and one cannot even conjecture how much is missing from the stone. To judge solely by what is broken off, the missing part is about 0.177 metres in height (6° 6′): thus the stone was originally at least 1.14 metres (3ds 6° 6′) high ...'⁶ In other words, 'about one fourth of the sole remaining part of the hieroglyphic text is missing, because of the truncation of the right and left sides, without mentioning all that is lacking above the first line, which may have amounted to half to two-thirds as much in addition'.

Before his death in 1810, Rémi Raige, who remained fascinated by the Rosetta Stone, had proposed having a separate engraving of the demotic inscription made, in order to make it easier to study. The editors of the *Description* adopted this idea. Thus a *gravure au trait* ('a kind of facsimile without shadows') was created that scrupulously reproduced every mark on the stela.

The demotic text was represented on sixteen plates, each reproducing two lines of the inscription. Each line was divided into four parts: Raige himself indicated where the divisions should be made; he maintained that they corresponded to the end of a word. The 'alphabet' he thought he had been able to establish was also reproduced.

The commission entrusted with publishing the *Description de l'Égypte* regretted that it 'could not add to these plates M. Raige's investigations as well as his alphabet: the manuscripts he left at his death have not been made available to us.' However, not too much importance was attached to this work: 'The alphabet itself is incomplete, and contains a few errors [...]. All the same, the Commission has considered that it should not deprive the public of this collection of plates, which were engraved long ago and may facilitate the study of one of the most precious monuments of Egyptian antiquity.'[7]

In its treatment of the script, the *Description de l'Égypte* – so precise in other areas – was already outdated when it was published. By the time the series of twenty-three volumes was finally completed in 1828, the hieroglyphic system had already been deciphered.

CHAPTER EIGHT

Åkerblad's 'alphabet'

WHILE HELLENISTS in several countries were examining the Greek inscription on the Rosetta Stone, two men – a Frenchman and a Swede – undertook a far more complex task: the deciphering of the Egyptian inscriptions on the stela.

The Frenchman, Antoine Isaac Silvestre de Sacy, was an internationally recognized scientist whom Napoleon would have been proud to take with him to Egypt a few years earlier: in the world of orientalism, this rather grumpy, unprepossessing man was considered a great authority, like Monge in mathematics or Berthollet in chemistry. But Silvestre de Sacy was not much of a traveller, and still less of an adventurer. It was only with difficulty that he was persuaded to go once to Genoa, to get some oriental manuscripts. He let young people sail the seas with Napoleon, and pursued his own career along the banks of the Seine.

The son of a Paris notary, Silvestre early displayed an extraordinary gift for languages. A Benedictine having taught him Hebrew from a prayer book, he went on to study Syriac, Chaldean, Arabic, Persian and Turkish – not to mention German, English and Spanish. He took a degree in law and in 1791 became one of the general commissioners entrusted with overseeing the production of currency. However, having doubts about the Revolution, he retired to Sacy, a village in the region of Brie, whose name he took. This allowed him to pursue his translation work and his research on Arab history and Persian antiquities. The creation of the École des langues orientales in 1795 brought him back to Paris as professor of Arabic. At the same time, he was an associate and then a member of the department of ancient history and literature of the Académie des inscriptions et belles-lettres, before assuming the chair of Persian at the Collège de France in 1806.

The Swede Johann David Åkerblad's career was entirely different. He was an amateur, who came to oriental studies indirectly through diplomacy. He became interested in oriental languages when he was assigned to the embassy in Constantinople. Numerous journeys around the Mediterranean basin allowed him to perfect his knowledge of Arabic before he was transferred to the Swedish consulate in Paris in the first decade of the nineteenth century. There he studied Coptic and attended lectures given by Silvestre de Sacy, who was five years his elder, and who gave him a copy of the inscriptions on the Rosetta Stone.

Silvestre de Sacy's method

The Minister of the Interior, Jean Chaptal, a chemist and member of the Academy of Sciences, asked Silvestre de Sacy to study the famous stela. Sacy began by examining the demotic inscription, using the following method: starting from words in the Greek inscription – 'god,' 'king,' 'son' – he looked for their equivalents in the Coptic, and then tried to identify the same words alphabetically in the Egyptian inscriptions. In this way he succeeded in locating the names 'Alexander', 'Alexandria', 'Ptolemy', 'Arsinoe' and 'Epiphanes'. He thought he might also have found 'Isis', 'Osiris' and 'Egypt', but erred in identifying the name of the Memphite god Ptah with the Greek word *theos* (god).

Plutarch, commenting on Egyptian writing, referred to

No. 3.

No. 4.

No. 5.   *No. 6.*

No. 7.   *No. 8.*

No. 9   *No. 10.*

The first names that Silvestre de Sacy identified in the demotic inscription: no. 3, Alexander; no. 4, Alexandria; no. 5, Ptolemy; no. 6, Arsinoe; no. 7, Epiphanes; no. 8, Isis; no. 9, Osiris, no. 10, Ptah.

twenty-five different letters. Silvestre de Sacy found many more letters in the demotic inscription. He attributed this apparent abundance to several factors: the existence of upper- and lower-case letters, which would double their number; the use of foreign letters intended to render lexical borrowings; the various forms that certain signs could take depending on their position in the word, as in Arabic, Syriac or Hebrew; and finally, the use of 'abbreviations or monograms'. Taken together, these observations suggested to him that 'the Egyptian inscription is not a literal translation of the Greek inscription'. This was correct, but it made the task much more complicated.

Silvestre de Sacy went no further. He gave up; in a short paper published in 1802,[1] he set forth in convoluted language the efforts he had made and his disappointments: 'It is not without reason, Citizen Minister, that it may seem to you surprising that the hope I had at first entertained, if not of entirely deciphering the Egyptian inscription on the precious Rosetta monument, at least of reading enough of its words to know with certainty what language it is written in, has not been realized.' He acknowledged that a more competent specialist in Coptic, working on the original, might be able to make further progress in deciphering the text. 'To whomever this precious monument is entrusted, I hope that the efforts of the scientists who work on it will be better rewarded than mine; and I shall witness their success with genuine satisfaction, even if they prove that I was mistaken about the values I thought I could assign to a very small number of the characters on this monument.'

The student's response

The same year, Åkerblad sent Silvestre de Sacy his *Lettre sur l'inscription égyptienne de Rosette*.[2] He thanked him for having sent him, two months earlier, a copy of the inscriptions on the Rosetta Stone, but pointed out that he did not agree with his

Åkerblad's alphabet.

conclusions. Indeed, between the results of the work he had just completed and the 'erudite conjectures' of his former professor, he saw a 'total difference'. Åkerblad discussed Silvestre de Sacy's alphabetical analysis of the names of Alexander, Ptolemy and Arsinoe, and refuted several of his hypotheses. He added to the list the names of Berenice and of the priests involved in the worship of the kings, several Greek words reproduced in the same form in the Egyptian inscription, and identified the name of Egypt: Kemi(t).

While Åkerblad said he considered his work as provisional and incomplete, his study none the less included two plates, one showing the words that were supposed to have made it possible to reconstitute the Egyptian alphabet, and the other showing the letters composing this alphabet, which was still incomplete and subject to correction. In this way, he hoped to make the initial results of his studies available to later researchers.

Silvestre de Sacy's reply was encouraging, despite his understandable reservations regarding certain details. However, the courtesy of this exchange of letters between the two men was deceptive. Their later correspondence with third parties threw a quite different light on their relations. 'I have not been so fortunate as to please the erudite orientalist,' Åkerblad wrote in January 1815. 'I have felt little desire to continue research that will interest no one after such a declaration made by one of the greatest French scholars.'[3] And Silvestre de Sacy wrote to the same correspondent: 'Despite the sort of approbation I accorded to M. Åkerblad's system, in the response I sent him, I still have very strong doubts concerning the validity of the alphabet he has constructed.'[4]

And so Åkerblad abandoned his attempt. As for Silvestre de Sacy, he was too busy with other matters to make any further effort to decipher the Egyptian inscription. However, he remained interested in the subject, and as Royal Censor from 1814 onward, he continued to arbitrate the main episodes in the history of the decipherment. Although, like Åkerblad, he was subsequently attracted again to the dream of deciphering the inscriptions, both men were in the future to play only the role of informed interlocutors.

Whatever rivalry their initial successes may have aroused, their work was closely connected. They laid the foundations for deciphering the demotic inscription by identifying groups of characters that corresponded to several Greek names. It was now known that this cursive script used alphabetic signs to transcribe foreign proper nouns. But that was not necessarily true for the other words. The two scholars committed the same error by reducing demotic to an alphabetic script.

CHAPTER NINE

Champollion goes to work

I N J U LY 1799 when the Rosetta Stone was discovered, Jean-François Champollion was not yet nine years old, but he was already surrounded by a legend: wasn't it said that he had taught himself to read by deciphering his mother's missal? Yet far from being first in his class, this son of a Figeac librarian seemed almost to be the dunce: poor at spelling, resistant to mathematics, he had a hard time submitting to primary school discipline. Fortunately, he was taken out of the school in the course of 1799 and handed over to a priest, Abbé Calmels, who had already taught his elder brother and godfather, Jacques-Joseph. This change allowed the boy to show his true potential: under the direction of this exigent teacher, he progressed very quickly. Soon he had mastered Latin, and was ready to move on to Greek.[1]

Jacques-Joseph had recently moved to Grenoble. He was very attracted to the land of the pharaohs, and it was said that he had dreamed of going with Napoleon to Egypt. It was to him that the issue of the *Courrier de l'Égypte* announcing the discovery of the Rosetta Stone was sent.[2] Did Jean-François see it? Probably. In any case, he soon joined his brother in Grenoble. Jacques-Joseph took him under his wing and remained his protector and mentor for the rest of his life.

In Grenoble, the young student was entrusted to the Abbé Dussert, the director of a respected school in the city. Very soon, he displayed an uncommon attraction to oriental languages. The priest gave him courses on Hebrew, and two years later helped him begin the study of Arabic, Syriac and Chaldean. This passion led his family to give Jean-François the nickname 'Seghir' ('little' or 'young' in Arabic). But everyone came to call him 'Champollion the younger' in order to distinguish him from his brother, who was known as Champollion-Figeac.

As secretary of the Académie delphinale, Champollion-Figeac became one of the closest collaborators of the Prefect of the department of Isère, Joseph Fourier. The latter had just returned from Cairo, where he had spent more than three years in the key post of secretary-general of the Institut d'Égypte. A noted physicist and mathematician, Fourier had no training as a historian or orientalist. None the less, he undertook to write the historical introduction to the *Description de l'Égypte*, a delicate task, since what he said was likely to disturb the Catholic Church by challenging Biblical chronology. For this reason, he collected a great many documents and received a large number of visitors. In 1804, Jean-François, who was introduced to him, saw at his home a reproduction of the Rosetta Stone.

Through Fourier, the Champollion brothers met several veterans of Egypt, such as dom Raphaël, a monk from the Middle East who taught dialectal Arabic at the École spéciale des langues orientales in Paris. In 1805, dom Raphaël taught Jean-François the rudiments of this discipline, and encouraged him to take an interest in Ethiopian. When dom Raphaël returned to Grenoble a year later, he brought Jean-François a Coptic grammar and documents on the languages of India. For his part, Fourier did all he could to help the young man whose academic life was dominated by his chief passion: the study of Egyptian. And he began to involve him in the work of the Académie delphinale.

Immersion in oriental languages

Jean-François Champollion finally completed his secondary-school studies on 27 August 1807. Five days later, he undertook to decipher Egyptian and to reconstitute the religion, history and geography of ancient Egypt, in a memorandum presented before Grenoble's Society of the Sciences and Arts, which accepted him as a member: 'By designating you as one of its members, in spite of your youth,' he was told, 'the Academy considers what you have achieved, but it has still greater hopes for what you will do! It is pleased to believe that you will fully justify its hopes, and that, should your works one day make you famous, you will recall that you received your first encouragement from our Society.' That speech had premonition.

The young man settled in Paris, in order to attend courses on Arabic and Persian at the Collège de France and at the École de langues orientales given by Silvestre de Sacy and Louis Langlès. He took advantage of his residence in Paris to consult the Coptic manuscripts at the Imperial Library and to make copies of them. Jean-François pinned all his hopes on this language: 'I want to know Egyptian as I know French, because my great work on the Egyptian papyri will be based on that language.' He attended a mass in Coptic celebrated at the church of St Roch, and encouraged by his old friend dom Raphaël, he frequented Egyptian circles in Paris. There he made the acquaintance of the Abbé Tersan, who brought him from London a copy of the Rosetta Stone.

A letter to his brother, dated 27 December 1807, gave some idea of the care lavished on the young student and the work schedule he maintained. On Mondays, for example: 'At a quarter past eight, I leave for the Collège de France, where I arrive at nine o'clock. You know that it's quite far away, on the Place Cambrai, near the Panthéon. From nine to ten, I attend Mr de Sacy's lecture. Since my course in Hebrew, Syriac and

Chaldean is taught at noon, on leaving my course in Persian I go immediately to Mr Audran's, who has offered to let me stay there from ten to noon on Mondays, Wednesdays and Fridays. He remains within the Collège de France. We spend these two hours talking about oriental languages. At noon, we come down and he gives his course in Hebrew. [...] On leaving his course at one o'clock, I cross Paris and go to the École spéciale to attend at two o'clock the course given by Mr Langlès, who gives me special attention; in the evening, we converse.'3

Not everyone appreciated Jean-François Champollion's unbridled enthusiasm and his growing ambitions. Despite Fourier's introduction, he was rather cooly received by certain members of the committee entrusted with publishing the *Description de l'Égypte*. The geographer Edme François Jomard considered him a young greenhorn who intended to produce a toponymic study of the Nile valley without ever having been there, whereas he himself had just written his own geographical commentary for the *Description*. Worse than that: having acquired a solid knowledge of several oriental languages, Jean-François Champollion could hardly wait to begin deciphering hieroglyphics. Jomard saw himself as the man for that job.

Coptic or the Stone?

Champollion-Figeac, Jean-François's elder brother, had long been interested in the Rosetta Stone. On 2 June 1804, he presented to Grenoble's Society of Sciences and Arts a *Dissertation* on the Greek inscription,4 which he had procured in facsimile. On 4 July 1807, he wrote to his younger brother, who was still in Grenoble: 'Don't be discouraged about the Egyptian text – this is the time to apply Horace's precept: a letter will lead you to a word, a word to a sentence, and a sentence to all the rest, and so everything is more or less contained in a single letter: keep working until I can check your work myself.[...] If you have tried my method of reading the inscription on the Rosetta Stone, tell me at what results you arrived.'[5]

Jean-François replied the following April: 'You advised me to study the inscription on the Rosetta Stone. That is precisely where I intend to begin.'[6] He was already able to discern the weaknesses of others who were working at the same task: 'I tell you in confidence that Åkerblad didn't know much Coptic. He himself admitted to Abbé de Tersan (who told me about it) that in spite of his alphabet and his great discoveries he could not read three words of the text in the Egyptian inscription. That proves that his work on the monument is as futile as that of Pahlin on the hieroglyphic part of the inscription. Thus we have to start again from the beginning; that is what I am now starting to see.' However, this did not prevent him from also asking his brother to send him 'Åkerblad's and Mr de Sacy's letter on the Rosetta inscription'.

But he was aware of the necessity of not trusting any assertion, no matter how judicious it might be, and to begin every argument at the beginning in order to be able to refute or to demonstrate what others assumed without being able to offer proof. Every day he noted down his own errors and slowly constructed the foundations of a new discipline.

In June, he wrote to Jacques-Joseph: 'I am going to try out your method of reading the Rosetta Stone. I am afraid that our efforts will be in vain, because our Coptic dictionaries include too few words to hope to produce a complete translation of all the Greek sentences in precisely Egyptian words.' And a few days later; 'The attempt made on the Egyptian text produced no result. [...] The proper nouns that I read as Åkerblad did (though differing in the manner of breaking up the simple letters) are not in exact concordance with the Greek text.'

While pursuing his study of the Rosetta Stone, Champollion was increasingly aware of Coptic's potential contribution to the understanding of the Egyptian. In this, he agreed with his teacher Silvestre de Sacy, for whom 'it is only with the help of the Coptic language that it will be possible to decipher in a satisfactory manner the ancient alphabetic script of the Egyptians, and only this decipherment, if it is achieved, can lead to the discovery of the value of the hieroglyphic characters.'[7] Åkerblad agreed: only the Coptic language, he wrote, would make it possible to explain the Rosetta Stone. 'The more works in Coptic we discover, the greater our chances of finding the words and expressions, heretofore unknown, that constitute one of the difficulties in deciphering the Egyptian decree.'[8]

Back in Grenoble in the autumn of 1809, Jean-François Champollion added to his already rich library of books on the Orient, and particularly on Coptic, while at the same time deploring the lack of lexicons and grammars. Fortunately, he found among the manuscripts at the Imperial Library in Paris a few Coptic grammars written by Arabs, which were far superior to those written by Europeans. He hastened to copy them.

Sounds to transcribe Greek names

Through the influence of his brother, Jean-François Champollion was named, at the age of nineteen, adjunct professor of ancient history at the Faculty of Letters in Grenoble. Henceforth, 'Seghir' could devote much of his time to his great project. On 7 August 1810, he presented to the Académie delphinale a paper entitled 'Écritures anciennes des Égyptiens', in which he refuted the theories of several of his celebrated predecessors, including Kircher, Warburton and de Guignes, particularly with regard to the affinities between Chinese and Egyptian. However, he noted that these two languages both use certain signs phonetically in order to transcribe foreign names.

The authors of the decree inscribed on the Rosetta Stone had written in Egyptian the ideas expressed in the Greek text. But how could they have written the Greek proper nouns, which did not express any idea in Egyptian? Only phonetic signs could make it possible to write these names. 'The inscription on the Rosetta Stone,' Champollion remarked, 'presents the Greek names of Ptolemy, Berenice, Arsinoe, Pyrrha, Areia, Diogenes, Aetes, Alexander, etc.; they could not be expressed in the hieroglyphic part of this monument if these hieroglyphs did not have the power to produce sounds.'

There he was touching on an essential point. But those thirty pages still contained contradictory ideas.

Silvestre de Sacy, his former professor, urged Jean-François Champollion not to expect too much from the study of the stela. 'I do not think', he wrote to the elder brother, 'that he ought to devote himself to deciphering the Rosetta Stone. Success in this sort of research is more often the effect of a lucky combination of circumstances than of persistent work that sometimes leads us to take illusions for realities.' With such principles, it is easy to understand why Silvestre de Sacy failed where Jean-François Champollion succeeded. The latter acquired an impressive knowledge of linguistics, philology, history and religion. Silvestre de Sacy's warning stimulated him more than it discouraged him.

An indefatigable worker, Champollion redoubled his efforts, for there was no lack of competitors. The most worrisome was Étienne Quatremère, his former fellow student at the Collège de France and the École spéciale. Recently appointed to the department of manuscripts in the Imperial Library, this young man, who was highly regarded in Parisian intellectual circles, was supported by Silvestre de Sacy. Hadn't he claimed to have read a large portion of the hieroglyphs on the stela? The book Quatremère published in 1808 was defined as a 'short dissertation, intended for publication in a literary journal', in which he set out to 'demonstrate the identity of the Coptic language with the ancient language of the Egyptians'.[9] He recognized that the idea was not new, but thought it had been insufficiently established and explored. This publication allowed him above all an opportunity to announce 'a much more considerable work, completed long ago', which was soon to be published.

The work in question was in fact published in January 1811.[10] Furious to have been beaten to the punch, Champollion published a few months later the introduction to his *Égypte sous les pharaons*, a brochure of sixty-seven pages that had been composed in October 1810 and included an 'Analytical Table of the Geography of Egypt under the Pharaohs'. Quatremère's criticism of this work was rather moderate,[11] but the competition between the two men was publicly displayed. Silvestre de Sacy sided with Quatremère, which did little to calm the situation.

Two sorts of signs

In 1812, Jean-François Champollion became secretary of the Faculty of Letters and the University's assistant librarian. He relentlessly pursued the objective he had set for himself. The letters he exchanged at this time with his fellow-student Jean-Antoine Saint-Martin allow us to follow some phases in his long and difficult search. He sometimes got ahead of himself: 'I shall begin by proving that the two-syllable words are words composed of two other words. This analysis of the Egyptian language incontestably gives me the basis of the hieroglyphic system and I shall prove it.' But his observations gradually took form: 'In the hieroglyphs, there are two sorts of signs: 1° the six alphabetic signs indicated; 2° a considerable but indeterminate number of imitations of natural objects.' Or again: 'A single hieroglyph, taken in isolation, has no value. They are arranged in groups.'

His knowledge of Coptic sometimes gave him a distorted view of the hieroglyphic system, which he saw at this time as 'entirely syllabic'. He wrote about Coptic: 'I have analysed this language so much that I am convinced I could teach its gram-

mar to someone in a single day. I have followed its most perceptible sequences. This complete analysis of the Egyptian
language incontestably yields the basis of the hieroglyphic system and I shall prove it. But hush ...'[12]

Along with the hieratic and demotic papyri, the inscriptions on the Rosetta Stone still occupied a central place in his
studies, but the only copy of the stela at his disposal, which
was far from perfect, complicated his task: 'I am still working
on my Rosetta inscription and the results are not coming as
fast as I should like.' His efforts up to this point had been
focused on the intermediate inscription, the one in demotic,
which he had tried to read by taking as his inspiration what he
knew of Coptic. At the same time, he was making progress in
conceiving a grammar.

The first two volumes of his book L'Égypte sous les pharaons[13]
finally appeared in 1814. In them, he was very lucid on many
subjects, such as the role that Coptic and the Rosetta Stone
ought to play in deciphering ancient Egyptian: 'The first step
to be taken, and no doubt the easiest, in this study whose object makes it so important, was the reading of the Egyptian text
of the Rosetta inscription: I have been fortunate enough to see
my efforts crowned by almost complete success; several passages of the Egyptian text are cited in the two volumes I am
publishing, while awaiting the moment when the order I have
adopted shall focus all my attention on this precious monument.' In fact, he made a few brief allusions[14] to the names
present on the Stone, but reserved the bulk of his observations
for the succeeding volumes. At this point, his work was based
primarily on the reports of European and Arab travellers, classical authors, the Description de l'Égypte and the numerous Coptic manuscripts that he had been indefatigably copying for
years.

Silvestre de Sacy, having assumed the position of arbiter,
commented: 'M. Champollion, who has just published two
volumes on the geography of ancient Egypt, and who has

worked a great deal on the Coptic language, also claims to have read this inscription. I certainly have more confidence in the learning and criticism of M. Åkerblad than I do in those of M. Champollion, but so long as they have not published their results, it is better to suspend judgement.'[15]

Åkerblad or Champollion? A third man was about to enter the stage and lend a new dimension to this unavowed competition.

CHAPTER TEN

Signed 'ABCD'

A T T H E beginning of the same year, 1814, Sir William Rouse Boughton, a wealthy collector, sent Thomas Young the papyrus fragments he had brought back from Egypt. Young was not the first person one might have thought of. At forty-one, he was practising as a physician in London, had taught natural philosophy and physics at the Royal Institution, and was reputed to know about everything. A musician and a passionate astronomer, the author of papers on the most diverse subjects – from the theory of tides to the framework of sea-going vessels – , he had perfected the use of the eriometre to measure corpuscles in the blood and the three-colour theory that explained problems in the perception of colours. His discovery of the interference of light was considered one of the most important advances in optics since the time of Newton.

Young's friend and biographer Hudson Gurney presents him as a prodigy even as an infant, who learned to read at the age of two and learned by heart, without difficulty, poems in English if not in Latin. Like Champollion's, Young's education was unconventional; he went from a school to a tutor, and taught himself by reading alone. Curious about everything, he became familiar not only with Italian and French, but also with Latin, Greek, Hebrew, Arabic and Persian. In addition to medicine, he was interested successively, but always seriously, in botany, zoology, entomology, optics, chemistry and mineralogy.

Again like Champollion, Young had the good luck to be able to rely on an unstinting sponsor: his maternal uncle, Dr Richard Brocklesby, an eminent London physician, followed his progress step by step and lent him active support throughout his life. When Champollion was young, Brocklesby encouraged him to continue his study of medicine, to be sure, but he also gave him an opportunity to show his translations of Greek texts to specialists in the field. Young was no doubt excessively eclectic, but this character trait was counterbalanced by a fierce determination to carry out his enterprises, a quality that was attributed to his Quaker upbringing. He started out from the principle that 'what one man has done, another can do', and believed in the value of effort as much as in that of perseverance.

Elected a Fellow of the Royal Society at the age of twenty-one, Thomas Young practised medicine in London while at the same time teaching natural philosophy and pursuing his research in physics. He travelled to France as the Duke of Richmond's physician, and during his stay there attended a meeting of the National Institute at which Napoleon was also present. On his return, he was appointed the Royal Society's secretary for external affairs, an office he retained until his death.

It was during this crucial period in his medical career that Young contracted the Egyptian virus. In 1814, he happened on fragments of an ancient papyrus. He was fascinated by the strange signs, and soon came to feel an irresistible need to understand them – the vocation of a code-breaker.

A 'conjectural translation'

Young quickly moved from these fragments of papyrus to the triple inscription on the Rosetta Stone. His attention was attracted by an article claiming that the unknown language on the stela, like that on the windings of Egyptian mummies, could be reduced to an alphabet consisting of approximately thirty letters. At that point he came across Åkerblad's *Lettre sur l'inscription égyptienne de Rosette*, and soon thereafter offered a few anonymous remarks on the papyrus fragments Boughton had presented to the Society of Antiquaries. The following summer, he took a copy of the inscriptions on the Rosetta Stone to his country house and set to work.

In August, he wrote to Silvestre de Sacy, 'I am very anxious to know if Mr Åkerblad has continued his attempts to decipher it [the Egyptian inscription]... If you are still interested in the subject, I shall have great pleasure in communicating to you the results of some attempts of my own, which have enabled me to obtain a literal translation of the greater part of the words, but without concerning myself with the value of the characters of which they consist; this mode of entering upon the investigation appearing to be by far the least liable to error.'[1]

Silvestre de Sacy, flattered and pleased by the English scholar's courtesy, was very encouraging: 'I shall receive with great interest and gratitude, Monsieur, your views on this precious monument, although I do not pretend I shall be able to offer you any new light on the problem'.[2] In October 1814, Young sent him a copy of his 'conjectural translation'. The following year, this translation appeared, anonymously, in *Archaeologia*, the Society of Antiquaries' bulletin,[3] as an appendix to a paper by Sir William Boughton, the collector to whom Young partly owed his vocation as a decoder. His results were described somewhat presumptuously: 'By an attentive and methodical comparison of the different parts with each other, I had sufficiently deciphered the whole, in the course of a few months, to be able to send a translation of each of the Egyptian inscriptions considered separately, distinguishing the contents of the different lines, with as much precision as my materials would enable me to obtain'.

This optimism was tempered later on: 'I was obliged to leave many important passages still subject to some doubt, and I hoped to acquire additional information before I attempted to determine their signification with accuracy.' With a certain distance, he acknowledged that having taken the first step, he thought the rest would be easy. But his experience with languages reminded him that 'a hieroglyphical language, to be acquired by means of the precarious aid of a few monuments, which have accidentally escaped the ravages of time and barbarism, must exhibit a combination of difficulties almost insurmountable to human industry'.[4]

Silvestre de Sacy's commentaries on his 'conjectural translation' were guarded. In a long letter dated 20 July 1815, [5] the French orientalist analysed the method used by Young: 'I can easily understand, Monsieur, that by comparing the number of lines in the Egyptian inscription with the number of the lines in the Greek inscription, you first established with a compass, so to speak, points corresponding approximately to each other in each of the two inscriptions; that having then noted the frequent recurrence of certain formulas, you discerned other, more numerous, less equivocal or almost certain relationships; that you determined the value of several series of characters, and recognized their correspondence with one or another word or series of words in the Greek inscription; that on this basis, with the help of proper names, you established the value of a relatively large number of letters; and finally, that these known letters offered you a way of finding other words belonging to the Coptic language ...'

However, Silvestre de Sacy expressed serious reservations: 'But what I do not understand is that when you arrived at this point, you were able, simply by conjecture, without reading the Egyptian text, and without explicating it with the help of Coptic, to recognize in the Egyptian inscription things that are not present in the Greek inscription ...' None the less, his conclusions were clearly positive: 'I must admit that your translation, conjectural though it is, seems very plausible ... I imagine that you have made further progress and are now reading at least a large part of the Egyptian text.'

How to identify words

Young, having discovered in turn the importance of Coptic, began to study it. He hoped thereby to 'be able to find an alphabet that would make it possible to read the demotic inscription at least in a related dialect'. The English scholar had to gradually abandon this idea, because he was forced to 'admit that such an alphabet will never be discovered, for the very good reason that it never existed'. Under the Sibylline pseudonym 'ABCD', he published the results of his observations on the nature and origin of the demotic script (which he called 'enchorial', after the Greek).[6]

Despite his determination to pursue his research on Egyptian, Young was concerned about his reputation as a physician, which he feared might suffer if he became publicly involved in too many unrelated activities. He therefore justified the anonymous publication of his initial results by referring to their modesty and by a sort of duty to maintain a certain reserve imposed on him by his status as a physician – from which he was able to free himself only a decade later, when he saw that he was about to lose the glory of having deciphered the hieroglyphics. Nevertheless, the energy and care he devoted to his philological research astonished his friends.

In 1816, he wrote two letters of particular importance – one to the archduke of Austria, the other to Åkerblad – concerning his progress in deciphering the hieroglyphs and the results he had achieved that paralleled those of Jean-François Champollion.[7] The following year, Young was received in Parisian scientific circles, where he met Baron Alexander von Humboldt, Arago, Cuvier, Biot and Gay-Lussac. He continued, however, to be interested in the most diverse subjects: in 1818, he was a member of a commission on weights and measures, and was named secretary of the Board of Longitude, with the responsibility of supervising the *Nautical Almanac*. He contributed to the *Supplement* to the *Encyclopaedia Britannica* in all sorts of domains. It was there that he set forth in 1819, in a twenty-page article entitled 'Egypt', the main lines of his work on Egyptian scripts.[8]

As he himself acknowledged, Young adopted the method tested by Silvestre de Sacy. It consisted in first counting the groups of signs that recurred most frequently in the demotic text and comparing them with the words having the same number of occurrences in the Greek text. In this way, Young thought, he could identify the basic words, such as 'god', 'king', 'priest' and 'sanctuary'. Then he commented on the groups of hieroglyphic and demotic signs that had been isolated in this manner – on the Rosetta Stone or on other Egyptian monuments – which he rearranged by categories or in tables. The examination of these tables was rather disappointing: of the 202 signs or groups of hieroglyphic signs he reproduced in an appendix, fewer than forty were more or less correctly identified. Trying to guess the value of the signs, he was right five times out of thirteen, and this led him, for instance, to read the epithet 'Autocrator' as 'Arsinoe' and to see the name 'Sesostris' in the cartouche of 'Psammetichus'.

Silvestre de Sacy, whom one could not accuse of ill-will towards Young, wrote to him: 'I am less convinced of the truth of the values you attribute to various characters, and of the way in which you read most of the words you think you have recognized. I do believe that one can often determine, as you have, the place that a given word in the Greek inscription occupies in the Egyptian inscription, as one would do for a purely hieroglyphic inscription; but then to state the value of the letters of which the word is composed, and to say how it should be read, to present it in an entirely different script, *hic labor, hoc opus est*'[9]

Extract from Thomas Young's tables comparing various groups of hieroglyphic signs occurring in documents drawn from several European collections.

(an expression that could be loosely translated as 'that's another ballgame!').

Seven more or less new conclusions

What contribution did Thomas Young actually make to deciphering the demotic inscription on the Rosetta Stone, and more generally, to deciphering Egyptian script? In 1823, he drew up a list of his conclusions. Here is how he saw the problem:

> – First, that many simple objects were represented, as might naturally be supposed, by their actual delineations; secondly, that many other objects, represented graphically, were used in a figurative sense only, while a great number of the symbols, in frequent use, could be considered as the pictures of no existing objects whatever; thirdly, that, in order to express a plurality of objects, a dual was denoted by a repetition of the character, but that three characters of the same kind, following each other, implied an indefinite plurality, which was likewise more compendiously represented by means of three lines or bars attached to a single character; fourthly, that definite numbers were expressed by dashes for units, and arches, either round or square, for tens; fifthly, that all hieroglyphical inscriptions were read from front to rear, as the objects naturally follow each other; sixthly, that proper names were included by the oval ring, or border, or *cartouche*, of the sacred characters, and often between two fragments of a similar border in the running hand; and, seventhly, that the name of Ptolemy alone existed on this pillar, having only been completely identified by the assistance of the analysis of the enchorial inscription.

These seven conclusions he claims to be his own: 'And, as far as I have ever heard or read, *not one* of these particulars has ever been established and placed on record, by *any other* person, dead or alive.'[10]

Were these new conclusions? In reality, several of them had already been formulated, and even demonstrated, such as the notation of numbers, the function of royal cartouches and the reading of the name Ptolemy.

Jean-François Champollion later acknowledged that Young was the first to imagine 'the existence of a few signs representing sounds, which he thought were used in writing in hieroglyphics the proper names of foreigners to Egypt'. He also credited Young with having 'been the first to seek, though without complete success, to give a phonetic value to the hieroglyphs composing the names "Ptolemy" and "Berenice".' None the less, he said, Young still had 'no well-defined conception of the existence or general nature of the phonetic writing, nor any certainty regarding the alphabetic or disyllabic value that he had attributed to eleven of the thirteen hieroglyphic signs that actually composed the names "Ptolemy" and "Berenice" the only ones that the English scholar tried to analyse'.[11]

This in no way diminishes Young's achievement. He lent new impetus to the process of deciphering Egyptian script at a time when it seemed to be losing momentum.

CHAPTER ELEVEN

Three related scripts

WHILE THOMAS YOUNG was exploring the re-
sources of his new hobby, Jean-François Champollion
experienced moments of extreme discouragement. It has to be
acknowledged that the turbulent history of France affected his
personal situation. On two occasions between 1814 and 1817,
the Dauphiné region had been invaded by foreign troops, causing the Faculty of Letters to be closed and courses cancelled.
The Champollion brothers, who had supported Napoleon during the Hundred Days – people called them 'Champoléon' –
were confined to their home in Figeac. This was a hard time for
them. When he returned to Grenoble a year and a half later,
Jean-Francois was able to obtain only a job as professor of
history and geography, and did not recover his post as assistant librarian until the autumn of 1819.

The restoration of the monarchy led to the re-establish-
ment of the old academies. The Académie des inscriptions et
belles-lettres regained its original name and its former permanent secretary, Bon-Joseph Dacier.[1] The elder Champollion,
who had been allowed to return to Paris, quickly became
Dacier's confidant. The Académie, of which he became a non-
resident member in 1818, gave a prize to his work, *Annales des
Lagides, ou chronologie des rois grecs d'Égypte successeurs d'Alexandre le
Grand*.

Throughout this period, both in Figeac and in Grenoble,
Jean-François continued to study and to work on his Coptic

dictionary and grammar. But he sought in vain to have them published by the Académie des inscriptions et belles-lettres. In July 1815, Silvestre de Sacy wrote a negative report on the two manuscripts, offering arguments that are not very persuasive.

'One of the British Museum's finest ornaments'

On 10 November of the preceding year, Champollion had sent his most recent work, *Égypte sous les pharaons*, accompanied by a long letter, to the president of the Royal Society in London.[2] He presented these two volumes as the first of a much larger enterprise: 'The part on geography is to be followed by one concerning the language and writings of the Egyptians. This second part will be the more important as well. It is also the one that presents the most problems to be solved and obstacles to be overcome. The basis of my work is the reading of the inscription in Egyptian characters that is one of the British Museum's finest ornaments; I refer to the monument found at Rosetta. The efforts I have made to this end have not been, if I may say so, entirely fruitless; and the results I believe I have achieved after long and continual study lead me to hope that I shall make still greater discoveries.'

In the same letter, he asks that various passages be checked, the copies available to him diverging in a number of places: 'I have two copies of this inscription; one is made from the facsimile that your society had engraved, and the other is the engraving of the same monument that is to be included in the third instalment of the *Description de l'Égypte*, published by order of the French government ... It must not be forgotten that more progress in [understanding] this essential part of Egyptian antiquity would have been made, as I have said, had a cast copy of the great monument of Rosetta been deposited in each of the main libraries of Europe and sent to its most celebrated academies ...'

It was Thomas Young, in his capacity as the Royal Society's secretary of external affairs, who replied to Champollion's letter: 'I have taken great pleasure and interest, Sir, in making the comparisons you desired to be made between the two copies of the inscription. In general, that of the Society of Antiquaries seems to me almost perfect; occasionally, however, the French copy is more exact: but in most of the places you mentioned, there is some obscurity in the original characters, which are rather vague or worn, and only by comparing the various parts of the stone can one arrive at the right reading.'[3] The two men were now in contact with each other; their dialogue was rather quickly interrupted after this initial exchange in 1822, but it later continued more or less regularly, depending on the circumstances, until Young's death.

'After having determined the meaning of several hieroglyphic characters,' Young wrote, 'I found a few of them very distinctly visible in our Egyptian inscription: thus it is certainly not simply alphabetic. Were it not for that fact, I have no doubt that Mr Åkerblad and yourself, Sir, who have studied Coptic in such depth, would already have succeeded in producing a translation more perfect than my own, which was drawn almost entirely from a very laborious comparison of its different parts, both with each other and with the Greek translation. If you would be so good as to indicate someone living in Paris who could deliver it to you, I should be honoured to give you a copy as a very inconsiderable mark of my esteem.'

Champollion was relieved on seeing the copies of the passages on the stela that were bothering him. 'The version you have given me,' he wrote to Young, 'justifies my conjectures regarding certain words whose value I guessed without being able to assign it ...'[4] As for Young's 'conjectural translation' of the demotic inscription, it was ultimately Silvestre de Sacy who lent Champollion a copy the following year.

A simplification of the hieroglyphs

In the spring of 1818, Champollion had still not succeeded in acquiring a better reproduction of the inscriptions on the Rosetta Stone. In a letter written on 19 April, he told his brother that if he could lay his hands on one he would solve the problem, adding somewhat boastfully: 'It is certain that with the Commission's engraving I would eventually succeed in placing under each hieroglyph the corresponding French word and even the cursive Egyptian; the Greek goes without saying. This is no great exaggeration, since this work is already three-quarters completed; I know where the hieroglyphic inscription begins and ends with regard to the cursive and the Greek. I shall prove that at least two-thirds of the inscription is missing ...'[5]

In June, he finally received copies made from impressions that allowed him to correct several passages in the copy he was working on. But he wanted more: 'I have examined the impressions or rather the proofs made from the Rosetta Stone, and I am convinced that they will be useful to me to some extent, but much less than I had imagined. Despite their imperfection, I have already seen that a correction I had seen fit to make in the fifth line of the hieroglyphic inscription is fully justified ... I may be able to use it to advantage in some other passages. The cursive part is much clearer than the hieroglyphic part, and the quick comparison I made with the Commission's engraving shows with what rigorous precision the Commission's drawings were made. This parallel convinced me of the importance of having in my possession a copy of the hieroglyphic part engraved by the Commission ...'[6]

At this same time, Champollion was beginning work on his *Essai d'un dictionnaire des hiéroglyphes égyptiens*, and on 19 August he sent a paper on this subject to the Académie delphinale. After an interruption of nearly two years occasioned by a very taxing workload, he thus returned to his favourite studies.

Although urged on by his elder brother, Champollion resisted the temptation to formulate hypotheses that were not based on a genuine understanding of the hieroglyphic system as a whole: 'I have already found the articles, the formation of plurals, and a few conjunctions, but that does not suffice to determine at this point the system of this script. The results of my work have already overturned all the ideas I had formed concerning the hieroglyphs ...' This was a defect he was inclined to point out in the works of Jomard and Young: 'I feel truly sorry for the poor English travellers to Egypt who are obliged to translate the inscriptions in Thebes using Dr Young's manual.'

During this period of reflection, Champollion considered all sorts of ideas, some of them insightful, others far-fetched, but he was as critical of himself as of others. He continued to take an interest in all the Egyptian documents he came across, particularly papyri covered with various kinds of signs. The first concrete evidence of his work concerned the three types of Egyptian script (hieroglyphic, hieratic and demotic), whose common points and specificities he commented on.

Thus before he left for Grenoble in April 1821, he was able to publish a fascicle consisting of seven pages and seven plates,[7] in which he summed up his conclusions:

> My comparisons have yielded the following results: 1st that the script in which Egyptian manuscripts of the second kind [hieratic] are written is not in any way alphabetical; 2nd that this second system is no more than a simple modification of the hieroglyphic system, and differs from it only in the form of its signs; 3rd that this second kind of script is the hieratic of the ancient Greeks, and should be considered a hieroglyphic tachygraphy [or shorthand]; 4th that the hieratic characters (and consequently those from which they derive) are signs of things and not sounds.

Champollion was mistaken in excluding any phonetic

dimension from Egyptian script. However, he was moving in the right direction when he asserted that hieratic script was only a cursive, simplified form of the hieroglyphic script, and that it functioned in accord with the same system.

He soon established that demotic was a still more abridged cursive form of the hieroglyphics, and generally governed by the same rules. The three Egyptian scripts were thus related, and to a certain extent derived from each other. Young had sensed this. Champollion proved it, thus taking an important new step towards deciphering Egyptian.

CHAPTER TWELVE

The letter to M. Dacier

H AVING LOST his posts as assistant librarian and professor at the Royal College, Jean-François Champollion
left Grenoble for Paris, where in July 1821 he took lodgings
close to the Institute, at no. 28 rue Mazarine, setting up his
study in the attic. After having defined the nature of hieratic
script,[1] he then turned to demotic, undertaking a new analysis
of the middle inscription on the Rosetta Stone. He wrote a
paper on this subject which he presented to the Académie des
inscriptions et belles lettres on three occasions during the
meetings of 23 August, 30 August and 20 September 1822. The
paper was very well received, even by Silvestre de Sacy, whom
during the preceding years Champollion had repeatedly
accused of being a charlatan.[2]

Up to that point, Champollion had hesitated for a long
time, and remaining loyal to his principle, abstained from
premature publication. He succeeded, not without difficulty,
in resisting those who tried to discourage him, as well as those
who urged him to conclude prematurely. However, beginning
in the summer of 1821, he felt he was on sure ground. Even if
the comparisons among hieratic, demotic and hieroglyphs
sometimes still led him into error when he relied too systemat-
ically on the principle of the linguistic identity of the three
forms of writing, this method was taking him in the right
direction. The comparative table of more than three hundred
hieroglyphic, hieratic and demotic signs he drew up testified

Pl. IV.

Tableau des Signes Phonétiques
des écritures hiéroglyphique et Démotique des anciens Égyptiens

Lettres Grecques	Signes Démotiques	Signes Hiéroglyphiques
A		
B		
Γ		
Δ		
E		
Z		
H		
Θ		
I		
K		
Λ		
M		
N		
Ξ		
O		
Π		
P		
Σ		
T		
Υ		
Φ		
Ψ		
X		
Ϫ		
ΤΟ ΤϪ		

J. F. Champollion the younger, Lettre à M. Dacier, 'Table of Phonetic Signs', plate IV.

to this by the small percentage of inexactitudes it contained.

By counting words and signs

On 23 December 1821, Jean-François Champollion celebrated his thirty-first birthday. A simple but luminous idea crossed his mind: to compare the various inscriptions on the Rosetta Stone wouldn't one have to count their respective signs? He counted. The fourteen more or less fractured lines of the hieroglyphic text corresponded to about eighteen complete lines of the Greek text. By extrapolation, that yielded 1,419 hieroglyphs for 486 Greek words. Three times as many. It was therefore impossible that each hieroglyph expressed by itself a single idea.[3] Did they represent sounds instead? The phonetic character of this script, which had been suspected by several researchers, including Champollion himself, was perhaps thereby confirmed. Another step in the right direction.

By drawing on his own knowledge, his own demonstrations founded not only on the Rosetta Stone but on all the documents of whose existence he was aware, Champollion was now able to discern the tentative principles that might lead to deciphering the script. The use of a constantly expanding body of documents allowed him to test what for his predecessors could only be unverifiable hypotheses.

Acknowledging the contributions made by Silvestre de Sacy's, Åkerblad's and Young's readings of the demotic inscription on the Rosetta Stone, Champollion credited them with having formulated 'the first precise ideas drawn from this monument'. But aware of his own contribution, he considered himself the sole competent authority with regard to the phonetic value of the signs they studied. 'It is from this same inscription,' he wrote, 'that I have deduced the series of demotic signs which, by assuming an alphabetic character, express in ideographic texts the proper names of persons foreign to Egypt.'

Champollion's observations regarding the equivalence of hieratic, demotic and hieroglyphic signs suggested to him that the 'pure hieroglyphs' followed the same rules as the demotic.

Therefore he had to find the same phonetic usage of a certain number of signs in order to write Greek and Latin proper names. This was how he read the name of Ptolemy on the Rosetta Stone. Beginning at the right, he identified the 'square' as the letter 'P', and the second sign, which he called 'segment of a sphere', as a 'T'. The third sign, which Young had designated as a 'knot', corresponded to the Greek omicron and to our 'O'. The lion was equivalent to the consonant 'L.' Champollion identified the following character as an 'M', the 'two feathers' or 'leaves' – these were later recognized to be reeds in bloom – as 'Y' and the 'curved mark' as an 'S': P + T + O + L + M + Y + S.

But the Rosetta Stone could not take him very far, since three-quarters of its hieroglyphic inscription was missing. Champollion therefore drew, with limitless curiosity and perspicacity, on other Egyptian documents that were to allow him to complete his demonstration.

The first of these was a little obelisk from the island of Philae, which had recently been taken to England. The Hellenist Jean Letronne sent Champollion a lithographic copy he had just received from the collector William Bankes: although the monument bore a Greek text on its base and hieroglyphic inscriptions on its upper part, Champollion immediately realized that this was not a genuinely bilingual document, but distinct inscriptions written in two different languages.[4] The hieroglyphic texts none the less contained Ptolemy's cartouche and that of Cleopatra. It was the latter's name that provided Champollion with the first signs of a pseudo-alphabet:

The first sign is a sort of quarter-circle and represents the letter 'K' ... The second, a recumbent lion, must represent the

'L' ... The third sign of Cleopatra's name is a feather or leaf that represents the short vowel 'E' ... The fourth character of

Cleopatra's hieroglyphic cartouche, which represents a flower with a curving stem, corresponds to 'O'. The fifth sign ... which has the form of a parallelogram and must represent the letter 'P', is also the first sign in Ptolemy's hieroglyphic name. The fifth sign corresponding to the vowel 'A'... is a hawk ... The seventh character is an open hand representing 'T' ... The eighth sign ... which is a mouth seen straight on, is the 'R' ... Finally, the ninth and last sign ... which has to be the vowel 'A' is in fact the hawk ...'

But why was the 'T' represented by an open hand in Cleopatra's cartouche, whereas in Ptolemy's it was a 'segment of a sphere'? Was the demonstration invalid? Sure of himself, Champollion thought the Egyptians might have used different hieroglyphic signs to express the same sound: he called them 'homophones', and went on with his research.

The documents copied from the great temple in Karnak provided Champollion with the cartouches of Ptolemaic and Roman kings – names written in phonetic hieroglyphs and known in a different form in Greek and Latin. The letters composing the names of Ptolemy and Cleopatra allowed him to identify others – Alexander, for instance – and to determine the graphic variants of certain sounds.

From that point on, the demonstration begun for demotic by Champollion's predecessors, was complete for the proper names of foreign origin transcribed in hieroglyphs: they could be retranscribed only in the form of signs expressing sounds. Each name newly identified made it possible to read other hieroglyphs. The sources Champollion had been collecting for years now revealed to him the signs making up the names of Berenice, Sabina, Caesar, Tiberius, Domitian, Vespasian, Trajan, Hadrian and Antoninus, as well as the titles 'Autocrator' and 'Caesaros'. As rudimentary as it was, this way of writing foreign names contained many indications regarding the phonetic value of certain hieroglyphic signs and how they worked.

Starting from the Greco-Roman period, Champollion moved further back in time. 'Phonetic writing,' he thought, 'existed in Egypt at a very early time. It was initially a necessary part of ideographic writing; it was then employed to transcribe the proper names of peoples, countries, cities, sovereigns and foreign individuals ...' Later on, Egyptians used the expression of sounds more frequently, but without giving up their ideographic scripts, which were made sacred by religion and by continual use over many centuries.

Ramses as well, and Thutmosis

The events immediately preceding the famous meeting of 27 September 1822 at the Académie des inscriptions et belles-lettres have become legendary. Thus it is difficult to reconstitute them in their authenticity. They were reported by Aimé, Jean-François's nephew and son of Jacques-Joseph.

On 14 September, reproductions of various reliefs from Egyptian temples that Jean-Nicolas Huyot had sent to Champollion suddenly allowed him to read the name of Ramses and that of Thutmosis, two of the most prestigious pharaohs in Egypt's history. Overcome with excitement, he rushed into his brother's office at the Institute to tell him the news, uttering the sentence that has become famous: 'I've got it!' (*Je tiens l'affaire!*). Then he collapsed, his emotion being too much for him. However, he was back on his feet by 20 September, when he read the next instalment of his paper on demotic at the Académie.

The text of the paper Champollion wrote for 27 September was first sent to Silvestre de Sacy. On the draft, the latter's name had been crossed out and replaced by that of the

Académie's permanent secretary, Bon-Joseph Dacier. The handwriting is not that of Jean-François, but that of his brother, Jacques-Joseph.[5]

Thus it was on 27 September 1822 that 'M. Champollion the younger also presented to the Académie his paper on the phonetic hieroglyphs and their use in the inscriptions on Egyptian monuments to transcribe the names, throne names and titles of Greek and Roman princes.'[6] The reading of an eight-page summary[7] took up most of the meeting. None the less, homage was also rendered to a certain number of scholarly works, and Jomard presented 'a manuscript map of the Siwa oasis and the roads leading to it'. Champollion's was one paper among others, but it left no one indifferent.

The *Moniteur universel* for 1 October announced the news to its readers: 'The latest paper presented to the Académie shows that certain hieroglyphs also acquire a phonetic value. M. Champollion the younger has discovered the alphabet, based on the monuments themselves; the signs that he has collected are equivalent to the vowels and consonants of the Greek alphabet; by applying them to the hieroglyphic inscriptions that decorate Egyptian temples, he immediately recognized on most of them the names of Alexander the Great, Ptolemy, Cleopatra and Berenice.'

Curious readers could consult the complete text of the *Lettre* the following month, in a forty-four page pamphlet accompanied by four plates. In it, Champollion wrote: 'The phonetic script of the Egyptians cannot be considered a system as fixed and invariable as our own alphabets. The Egyptians were used to representing their ideas directly; in their ideographic script the expression of sounds was merely an auxiliary instrument; when the occasion to make use of them arose more often, the Egyptians resorted to them to express sounds, but did not give up their ideographic scripts, which were hallowed by religion and by their continual use over many centuries.' This was a claim that he later qualified, having

M. Champollion, jeune, termine la lecture de son mémoire sur
l'écriture démotique ou populaire des Égyptiens.

M. abel Remusat continue également la 2.e lecture de
son second mémoire sur les relations politiques des Princes D'Europe,
et particulièrement des Rois de france avec les Empereurs mongols.

M. Dureau de lamalle fait la 2.e lecture de son
mémoire sur les sièges de Samos et de Platée.

Séance levée.

Séance du Vendredi 27. 7bre 1822.

à laquelle ont assisté: MM. Daunou, Dureau de lamalle,
Lanjuinais abel Remusat, amaury Duval, St Martin,
Gail, Petit Radel, Langlès, Monger, Raoul Rochette,
quatremère de quincy, Caussin, Naudet, Chezy, quatremère
Walckenaër, De Gérando, Boissy, Barbié Dubocage,
Bétencourt, Silvestre de Sacy, Arial, Boissonade,
Dacier, Jomard.

Le procès verbal de la séance précédente est lu, l'a rédaction en est
adoptée.

M. L'abbé Reynaud fait hommage à l'académie d'un exemplaire
De ses extraits arabes traduits pour faire suite aux historiens des
Croisades. Dépôt à la bibliothèque et remerciement à l'auteur.

Une lettre de M. Monnier, Conservateur du Musée du Jura, et
annonçant de nouveaux dessins de sa composition, est renvoyée à la Comm.^{on}
Des antiquités nationales.

M. abel Remusat communique à l'académie un extrait d'une lettre
Du Conseil de la société biblique britannique et étrangère, annonçant un
nouvel envoi de bibles en divers langages destinés à l'institut.

M. Champollion le jeune, communique également à l'académie
un mémoire sur les hiéroglyphes phonétiques et sur leur emploi dans
les inscriptions des monuments Égyptiens, pour y transcrire les
noms, surnoms et titres des Princes Grecs et Romains.

M. Jomard met sous les yeux de l'académie une carte manuscrite
De l'oasis de Siwa et des routes qui y conduisent.

M. de Sacy dépose sur le bureau le 3.e numéro du Journal asiatique
Dépôt à la bibliothèque.

Extract from the transcript of the meetings of the Académie des inscription et des
belles lettres on 20 and 23 September 1822.

gradually recognized the considerable role played by phono-grams in this script.

In the *Lettre à M. Dacier*, Champollion was still marked by the prejudices of the time. He claimed that Egyptian scripts were essentially 'ideographic', and that they depicted 'ideas, not sounds'. The need to render Greek and Roman names was supposed to have led the ancient Egyptians to make exceptions to their system.

Nevertheless, the man who had just deciphered the names of Ramses and Thutmose knew that phonetic writing had been used long before the Greco-Roman period. He knew it, but did not yet dare to assert it too openly. The end of his *Lettre* was as allusive as it was prudent: 'I am sure that the same *phonetic-hieroglyphic* signs used to represent the sounds of Greek and Roman proper names were also used in ideographic texts in-scribed long before the Greeks and Romans arrived in Egypt, and that they already had, in certain cases, the same value representative of sounds and articulations ... The elaboration of this important and decisive fact is part of my work on pure hieroglyphic writing. I could establish it in this letter only by going into extraordinary detail. I believe, Monsieur, that phonetic writing existed in Egypt in a very distant age; that it was initially a necessary part of ideographic writing.'

Thus in his *Lettre à M. Dacier*, Champollion did not say every-thing he knew or suspected. He revealed only the discovery of an 'alphabet of phonetic hieroglyphs initially applied to Egypt-ian monuments of the Greek and Roman period alone'. He did not go nearly as far as his hypotheses went, because he wanted to verify them before presenting them to the scholarly world.

Although a decisive step had been taken towards deci-phering the hieroglyphics, many more remained, and they were no easier. Champollion now had to deal with Egyptian it-self, and no longer with its ancillary applications; in short, he had to get to the heart of the problem. But to do that, he needed inscriptions, more inscriptions, ever more.

CHAPTER THIRTEEN

Ideas and sounds

THE PRUSSIAN geographer and naturalist Alexander
von Humboldt was present at the reading of the *Lettre à M.
Dacier*. He regularly attended the meetings of the Académie des
inscriptions, of which he was soon to become a member, and
since his return from a long voyage in South America, lived
only a stone's throw away from the Institute, at no. 3 quai
Malaquais. At his request, Champollion gave him a copy of the
text before it was published, so that von Humboldt could give
it to his brother Wilhelm, a linguist and philosopher with a
European reputation, and a friend of Goethe and Schiller.

Wilhelm von Humboldt examined Champollion's arguments with great care, and sent him in return the manuscript
of his *Mémoire sur les hiéroglyphes phonétiques de M. Champollion le
Jeune*. The two scholars continued to exchange views in a regular, cordial manner through the intermediary of Alexander, but
they never met.

The *Lettre à M. Dacier* was honoured in April 1823, during a
session of the Société asiatique which had just been established under the presidency of Louis-Philippe, duc d'Orléans,
and of which Alexander von Humboldt was one of two vice-
presidents, François René Chateaubriand being the other. 'The
brilliant discovery of the hieroglyphic alphabet is honourable
not only for the scholar who made it, but for the Nation,' the
duc d'Orléans proclaimed. 'It should make us proud that a
Frenchman has begun to penetrate these mysteries that the

Ancients revealed only to a few well-tested adepts, and to decipher these emblems whose meaning all modern peoples had despaired of discovering.'[1]

Thomas Young's fair play

Thomas Young, in Paris to hear Fresnel discuss the theory of light, was also present at the meeting held at the Institute on 27 September 1822, where he witnessed the success of his young rival. The English physician found himself in a doubly ambiguous situation. Though he was associated with the discovery and acknowledged by Champollion as one of his precursors, Young's achievements were none the less indirectly devalued by the tacit comparison implicit in the Lettre. Above all, he was deprived of the starring role.

At first, he was carried away by enthusiasm, as was shown by the letter he wrote on 29 September to William Richard Hamilton, the man who had seized the Rosetta Stone in Alexandria: 'I have found here, or rather recovered, Mr Champollion, junior, who has been living for these ten years on the inscription of Rosetta, and who has lately been making some steps in Egyptian literature, which really appear to be *gigantic*. It may be said that he found the key in England which has opened the gate for him, and it is often observed that *c'est le premier pas qui coûte;*[2] but if he did borrow an English key, the lock was so dreadfully rusty that no common arm would have had strength enough to turn it; and, in a path so beset with thorns, and so encumbered with rubbish, not the first step only, but every step, is painfully laborious; especially such as are retrograde; and such steps will sometimes be necessary: but it is better to make a few false steps than to stand quite still.'[3]

Young described in detail the content of Champollion's paper and concluded, writing as someone who knew the field, with one of the finest encomiums the Frenchman ever

The fort at Abukir, flying the French flag.

A house near Rosetta.

A view of the interior of Hassan Kachef's palace in Cairo, where the Institut d'Égypte held its meetings. The Rosetta Stone was brought there shortly after its discovery, in August 1799.

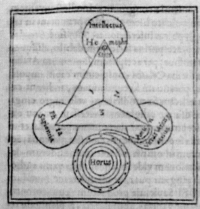

Atq, ex his apparet & omnibus manifeſtum ſit, Sacroſanctam & terbenedictam illam Triadem Fidei Chriſtianę myſterium, vti maximum, ſic ter ſublime, nullo non tempore, etiam ſub obſcuris fabularum figmentis adumbratum eſſe.

Quod porrò Oſiris nihil aliud ſit, quá primus intellectus, Sol ille æternus, ac primus rerú omniú productor, qui per Iſidem coniugem ſapientiam ſuá Horum, mundú videlicet produxerit, Hieromátę varijs Hieroglyphicorum ſchematiſmis indicabant, quemadmodum columnæ multis in locis erectæ teſtátur, vnius celebrem inſcriptionem Authores reſerunt his verbis.

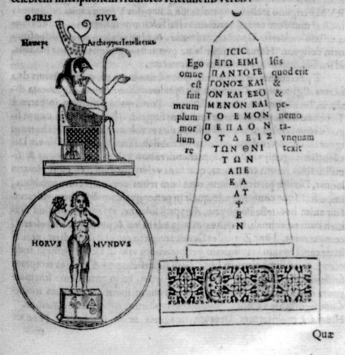

ICIC
Ego | ΕΓΩ ΕΙΜΙ | Iſis
omne | ΠΑΝΤΟ ΓΕ | quod erit
eſt | ΓΟΝΟΣ ΚΑΙ | &
fuit | ΟΝ ΚΑΙ ΕΣΟ | &
meum | ΜΕΝΟΝ ΚΑΙ | pe-
plum | ΤΟ ΕΜΟΝ | nemo
mor | ΠΕΠΛΟ Ν | ta-
lium | ΟΤ Δ ΕΙΣ | vnquam
re | ΤΩΝ ΘΝΙ | texit
 | ΤΩΝ
 | ΑΠΕ
 | ΚΑ
 | ΑΥ
 | Ψ
 | Ε
 | Ν

OSIRIS SIVE
Hemept Archetypus Intellectus.

HORVS MVNDVS

Quæ

A far-fetched explanation of Egyptian religion by the German Jesuit, Athanasius Kircher (1602–1680).

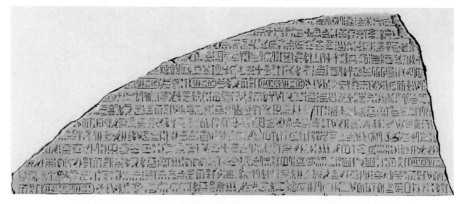

The hieroglyphic inscription, as published in the Description de l'Égypte, based on two casts, one in sulphur, made in Cairo, and the other in plaster, made in London.

The demotic inscription. Nothing is missing on the left side, and the truncation of the right side is minor compared with that of the hieroglyphic text.

The Greek inscription. The truncation of the lower right part of the inscription is equivalent to about one-fifteenth of the text. In the body of the inscription, the fractures and natural irregularities of the stone have been imitated as closely as possible.

Thomas Young (1773–1829). Trained as a physician and physicist, and with an encyclopaedic mind, he began to take an interest in Egyptian writing only at the age of 41. His work dealt chiefly with the Rosetta Stone, on which he identified words or groups of hieroglyphic signs, but without advancing so far as Champollion.

Antoine Isaac Silvestre de Sacy (1758–1838). A well-known linguist, professor at the Collège de France and at the École des langues orientales in Paris. He attempted to decipher the demotic inscription on the Rosetta Stone, and was able to identify a few proper names. He played the role of arbiter – seldom in a neutral manner – among the scholars seeking to decipher it.

Jean-François Champollion (1790–1832). Before being recognised as 'the decipherer of the hieroglyphs,' this bookseller's son from Figeac – tirelessly aided by his brother – had to overcome many obstacles and criticisms. He owed his success to hard work and an excellent knowledge of eastern languages, especially Coptic.

Edme François Jomard (1777–1862). This geographer and engineer was a member of the Commission on the Arts and Sciences established by Napoleon. On his return to France, he was elected secretary and subsequently commissioner for the publication of the Description de l'Égypte. Champollion always saw in him an adversary who opposed his election to the Académie des inscriptions et belles-lettres.

The Rosetta Stone in 1998, after being cleaned in the laboratory of the British Museum.

received: 'You will easily understand that even if I suffered some envy, I none the less felt nothing but joy at M. Champollion's success: my life is, as it were, extended by the entry of a young colleague into my research, someone who is at the same time much better versed than I in the different dialects of the Egyptian language. I sincerely wish his merits to be appreciated at their true value by his compatriots and by his government ... I promised him for his research all the assistance that I am able to provide him in England, and I expect from him in return that he will quickly send me all his future observations.' At this point, Young's sincerity was not in doubt.

The initial result was a series of visits in the course of which we can easily imagine the two men, both taking a passionate interest in their subject, exchanging opinions and documents, sometimes at no. 28 rue Mazarine, which Young visited on several occasions during his stay in Paris, and sometimes at Young's rooms, where Arago took Champollion. For several months, the two men pursued these animated discussions by correspondence, each trying to convince the other, inquiring about the slightest news in relation to the progress of the decipherment, asking each other for Egyptian texts that had not yet been examined.

Thus Champollion wrote to Young, after having sent him two copies of the Lettre: 'I should like to believe that certain doubts that you seem to have had concerning the transcriptions I give of the names of various Roman emperors have grown weaker on reading my little printed work, and that these same doubts will disappear altogether when you apply my phonetic alphabet to the proper names copied on the Egyptian monuments of the second and third styles, which must exist in Mr Bankes's rich collection.'[4] In this same letter, dated 23 November, Champollion demonstrated for the first time in writing his reading of the names of Ramses and Thutmosis.

However this cordial exchange between Champollion and Young did not last long. Translated into several languages, the

I cannot in fact resist the conviction that forces me, so to speak, to recognize in this cartouche, which appears so frequently, with these variations,

(and which you provisionally attributed to Maenuphthes), all the elements of the name *Ramses*.

This examination regularly yields the following transcription: Pʜɛɛcc, which we pronounce *Ramesès, Ramessè (s)*, or *Ramsès*, with the various Greek and Roman authors who cited this name that was so famous in Egypt. I ask you observe as well that this analysis of the name *Ramessès* corroborates in a singular way what you proposed regarding the hieroglyphic name of *Thouthmosis*, and confirms, so to speak, this interpretation, since this proper name is formed of the tropic sign of the god *Thoth*

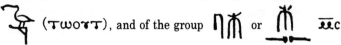

which gives Tⲱⲟⲩⲧⲙⲥ, from which the Greeks derived *Theth-mos-is* or *Thuthmos-is*.

Two extracts from Champollion's letter to Young, 23 November 1822.

Lettre à M. Dacier aroused many reactions. Champollion was attacked from various angles. Some writers sought to show that he had not contributed anything new, while others felt the need to bring together unpublished documents that might advance the decipherment of the hieroglyphics. Urged on by well-intentioned friends, Young himself feverishly set about writing a book. A few months before the latter appeared, an anonymous article in the *Quarterly Review* upset Champollion. He immediately wrote to Young: 'You know, Sir, the value I put on my relations with you, both for personal reasons and in the interest of science. I do not believe that you accept the anonymous author's assertions; and my esteem for your character is too profound for me to hesitate even an instant in communicating to you my feelings on this subject.'

While Young's response remained courteous, it showed that the rivalry between the two men finally won out over their recent friendship: 'The author of the article on your work analysed the object of his criticisms as poorly as he did what I had studied a few years earlier, and assuredly he has done neither of us justice. In addition, I refer to my book regarding my alphabet; as for yours, I have nothing to do with it. I have taken care to distinguish what is mine by citing the places where I have published it; I do not deny that you were able to arrive at the same results without having been acquainted with mine.'

A few months later, Young published, this time under his own name, a work with a revealing title: *An Account of Some Recent Discoveries in Hieroglyphical Literature and Egyptian Antiquities Including the Author's Alphabet, as Extended by Mr. Champollion, with a Translation of Five Unpublished Greek and Egyptian Manuscripts.* Whether or not he was convinced by the discoveries made by his rival, Young claimed his share of the honour, without really distinguishing between his conjectures and the work he was currently pursuing. The demonstrations sent him by Champollion as previews seemed to leave him cold: 'He is disposed to refer the name, which I consider as that of the father of

Amasis, to Sesostris, as synonymnous with Ramesses ...'⁵ Not having succeeded in isolating the signs that composed these different royal names, and seeking to divine their identity using his 'conjectural' method, Young confused sovereigns who lived more than a century apart.

Despite a certain reticence, he none the less acknowledged that his young colleague was the only one, apart from himself, who had carried out serious research on the subject, whereas others amused themselves with their little hypotheses: the French mathematicians with their calculations, the English metaphysicians with their unprovable theories. But this book was for Young a sort of last-ditch stand, since in the same year he wrote to a correspondent: 'Champollion is doing so much that he will not suffer anything of material consequence to be lost ... For these ... reasons I have now considered my Egyptian studies as concluded.'⁶

From monument to monument

Henceforth, Champollion had to follow through to the end the process on which he had embarked and develop his view of the hieroglyphic system. After having read several papers before the Académie des inscriptions et belles-lettres, which now supported every stage in his research, he began to explore the potentialities of his alphabet.

He moved forward one step at a time. Having determined the names of the Ptolemaic kings and Roman emperors, he attempted to read the names of private individuals, first Greeks and Romans, and then Egyptians. Next, he focused on the royal epithets that appeared on obelisks, and then on the names of the pharaohs, before finally attempting the first scientific description of the system of hieroglyphic writing. At this point the Rosetta Stone was only one element among others. The decipherment of the hieroglyphics had begun, and its results grew with the diffusion of the inscriptions available in France.

Champollion had worked on the epigraphic material from the Greco-Roman period. He now had to take an interest in earlier periods and establish the chronology of the pharaohs. In response to an anonymous critic who challenged him to read, using his method, the name of Cambyses (who conquered Egypt in 524 BCE), Champollion deciphered ... that of Xerxes, one of Cambyses's successors.

Next, Champollion analysed the main elements of the royal titulature. He was wrong about the meaning of the bee, following a reed, in the title of 'King of Upper and Lower Egypt', but he correctly identified the title 'son of Re', which began the second cartouche. With the help of the chronology of the Egyptian kings established by Manetho, and thanks to his vast knowledge of classical culture, Champollion was able to recognize the names of Nepherites and Hakoris (Twenty-ninth Dynasty) on the bases of two sphinxes in the Royal Museum, the name of Psammetichus I (Twenty-sixth Dynasty) on a Roman obelisk, the name of Osorkon (Twenty-second Dynasty) on a Heliopolitan obelisk, and so on. From monument to monument, from king to king, he worked his way backwards in time, with greater or less success depending on the difficulties he encountered, and thereby demonstrated the universality of the principle in accord with which he was working.

To move further ahead, the only path open to him consisted in amassing a body of inscriptions and studying them, each one contributing something that would help in interpreting the others. In 1822, Thomas Young had launched, by subscription, the collection of a corpus of texts,[7] and he had sent Champollion a copy of the first fascicle. Fourteen pages of it were devoted to a tentative parallel between the three inscriptions on the Rosetta Stone.

Champollion's reply was prudent and sensible: 'I have seen, by making a rapid examination of your comparison of

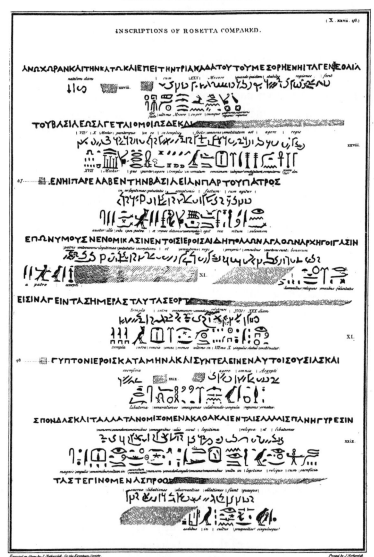

PILLAR OF ROSETTA.

A tentative parallel layout of one passage in the three inscriptions on the
Rosetta Stone, by Thomas Young (Hieroglyphics, p. 28)

the three texts on the Rosetta Stone that the similar paper that I presented to the Académie des inscriptions et belles-lettres a year ago agrees with yours on a great many points relating to the division and the value of the groups of characters, both hieroglyphic and demotic, but they differ fundamentally on many other points, whether regarding division or meaning.' For his part, he did not plan to publish a comparison of the three texts. 'I shall do so,' he wrote, 'only when I can add to all the demotic groups their equivalent in Coptic letters, as we can already do for proper names, whether Greek or Egyptian, and place under each hieroglyph its pronunciation, if it is phonetic, and its value, if it is not.'

In 1824, two years after the *Lettre à M. Dacier*, Champollion published his *Précis du système hiéroglyphique des anciens Égyptiens*. In this work, he explained that the hieroglyphs express 'sometimes ideas, sometimes sounds'. And in a magisterial manner, he summed up his thought: 'Hieroglyphic writing is a complex system, a script simultaneously figurative, symbolic and phonetic, in one and the same text, in one and the same sentence, and, I should say, almost in one and the same word.'

The essential point had thus been made.

CHAPTER FOURTEEN

A science is born

APPOINTED CURATOR of the Louvre's Egyptian collection on 14 May 1826, Champollion was thereafter to devote himself to enlarging the corpus of hieroglyphic inscriptions, which was the necessary precondition for pursuing their decipherment. He acquired, in the name of the king of France, the collection of the English consul in Egypt, Henry Salt, and was soon able to realize his old dream: to travel to the land of the pharaohs. A French-Tuscan expedition was organized together with Ippolito Rosellini in order to expand the collections of the Louvre and the museum in Turin. Among the twenty objectives of this journey, we read in the fifteenth position: 'It is of the most urgent interest for historical and philological studies to look for bilingual decrees among the ruins of ancient Egypt, such as the one on the Rosetta Stone. These stelae exist in great numbers in the Egyptian temples of all three orders. Excavations will therefore focus on these temples in order to find such monuments, which would help us make an immense step forward in deciphering hieroglyphic texts.'

The battle for another stela

On the periphery of this expedition, a final, almost anecdotal duel between the French and the English was to take place – over a bilingual stela, in fact. The latter had been found in a

Cairo mosque in September 1800, by an engineer working for the French office of Ponts et Chaussées. Having been taken to one of the Institut d'Égypte's palaces, it remained there when the French forces retreated.

Thomas Young found out about this stela by reading a book by an English traveller, Edward Clarke. Clarke was fulsome in his praise; describing the pieces of the stela piled up in the palace in Cairo, this lover of antiquities mentioned 'a very large slab, covered with an inscription in hieroglyphic characters, similar in every respect to the famous trilingual stone presently deposited in the British Museum'.[1] Questioned by Young in the spring of 1815, Jomard confirmed the existence of this stone; according to him, it was in very poor condition, but was worth transporting to Europe.

Young then addressed himself to the English consul in Egypt, Henry Salt, who was himself a knowledgeable antiquarian.[2] Several years went by without any news about the stela. In 1822, Young asked the son of one his friends, James Burton, who was in the service of Mohammed Ali, to look for the object.[3] Burton made a scrupulous search. For four years, every time he had an opportunity, he wandered about the Nasrieh quarter, hunting for the famous stela.[4] In 1826 he finally found it, in the Yakur mosque, where it was being used as the highest step on a rickety staircase. In order to lay hands on it, Burton offered bribes to four persons, without success. The question was ultimately referred to Mohammed Ali, who rendered a favourable judgement.

Young was very hopeful, and wrote to Baron Humboldt: 'Mr Burton [...] has been negotiating with the Pacha for its removal. From its magnitude and state of preservation, there is every reason to believe that it will rival the pillar of Rosetta in importance ...'[5] Young declared that it was absolutely necessary for him to complete his 'enchorial [demotic] lexicon'.

However, shortly afterwards the English consul was politely informed by the palace that it would not be possible to remove the stela. Salt did not renew his request. No doubt he had other concerns that he regarded as more important.

In September 1828, while passing through Cairo, Champollion went to see the stela in the mosque. Since the French consul in Alexandria, Drovetti, was ill, Champollion wrote to the acting consul: 'Please tell M. Drovetti that this stone that is being used as a doorsill for a small mosque in Cairo is in fact a triple inscription in hieroglyphic characters, in demotic and in Greek; only a very small part of it is visible on the long side [...]. The possession of such a monument would be a treasure for science. It has been refused, it is said, to the English consul; that is good. But it has not been refused to the consul general of France; this would be a notable and important victory over British arrogance, and an excellent opportunity to console France for the painful loss of the Rosetta monument.'

Drovetti, a great collector of antiquities, made it his duty, despite his illness, to deprive the English of the Cairo stone. And he succeeded. When he was about to leave Egypt, the antiquarian consul arranged for the stela to be added to the list of presents that Mohammed Ali was giving to King Charles X. Burton, furious to have lost when he was so close to winning, was able to obtain only a copy 'for His Majesty the King of England'.

The Cairo stone went to the Louvre.[6] However, once it was removed, it was noticed that it represented only half of the original stela. On it were the remains of a text known as 'the Decree of Canopus', issued during the reign of Ptolemy III (247–221 BCE). In the hieroglyphic inscription, the name 'Berenice' was barely discernible. The demotic part of the inscription was the best preserved, but most of its characters were illegible; others appeared only when the light struck them from certain angles. 'After all,' Burton consoled himself, 'I tried very hard and worried about an object which, I fear, may be of little use. Had it been complete, the stela would have been the most magnificent, the most priceless of treasures ...[7]

'Our alphabet is right'

Champollion, who had left Cairo for Upper Egypt, travelled from marvel to marvel. As he stood before each monument, he was able to verify his hypotheses. The French-Tuscan expedition filled boxes of notes and drawings. On the first of January 1829, Champollion sent from Wadi-Halfa, far in the south, a triumphant letter to M. Dacier: 'I am proud, now that I have followed the course of the Nile from its mouth to the second cataract, to be able to tell you that there is nothing that needs modification in our *Lettre sur l'alphabet des hiéroglyphes*. Our alphabet is right: it has been applied with equal success, first to Egyptian monuments from the time of the Romans and the Ptolemaic rulers, then, and this is far more interesting, to the inscriptions in all the temples, palaces and tombs of the pharaonic epochs.'

After sixteen months in Egypt, Champollion returned to France with an immense harvest. Rosellini naturally urged him to complete the publication of the monuments collected during their expedition, but Champollion gave priority to his *Grammaire égyptienne*. However, this volume appeared only after his death, when it was published by his elder brother. This colossal work concluded Champollion's decipherment of the Egyptian hieroglyphs. In nine chapters, he dealt successively with the form, categories, nature and interpretation of hiero-glyphic signs, and then went on to discuss at length the representation of common nouns and their determinatives, proper nouns (gods, private individuals, Egyptian and foreign sovereigns, countries, cities) and their determinatives, and the expression of the plural. Finally, he established the primary morphological and syntactical constituents of articles, pronouns, nouns, and numbers. This ambitious project, which Champollion had spoken of for so long, ultimately took form in less than ten years.

On 12 March 1831, a royal order addressed to the Collège

de France's administrator, Silvestre de Sacy, stipulated that 'a chair of archaeology is created in the Collège de France. M. Champollion the younger, member of the Institute, is named to this chair as professor.' The new course of lectures was announced in these terms: 'M. Champollion will set forth the principles of Egyptian-Coptic grammar, and he will develop the whole system of the *sacred writings*, by explaining all the grammatical forms used in *hieroglyphic and hieratic* texts.' This chair not only crowned a whole life of research, which the Académie had already honoured the preceding year by admitting Champollion as one of its members; in addition, it officially founded a new scientific discipline by according it at the same time its letters of nobility and the most prestigious of settings.

Champollion's career at the Collège de France was short. Exhausted by his work, suffering from diabetes and a disease of the liver as well as from galloping consumption, he died on 4 March 1832, in Paris, at the age of forty-one. Egyptology had hardly been born when it became an orphan.

CHAPTER FIFTEEN

Decipherers by the hundreds

T HE DISCOVERY of the Rosetta Stone in the last year of the eighteenth century made ancient Egypt more fascinating than ever. Everyone was aware that access to this civilization, whose antiquity and richness can be sensed without the need for commentary, would be by way of its writing. During all the stages in the rediscovery of this dead language, in Europe both scientists and scholars as well as amateurs more or less distant from the subject discovered a vocation to be decipherers. The deciphering of the hieroglyphs was experienced as a kind of Icarian dream, and the Stone as its mysterious symbol. Let us not forget that the Rosetta Stone was found in the heyday of romanticism.

In 1804, a Swedish diplomat very keen on orientalism, Nils Gustav Palin, published an *Analyse de l'inscription en hiéroglyphes du monument trouvé à Rosette*.[1] As the author himself acknowledged, this was a book written in one week, in order to 'communicate to the public the ideas that occurred to him when this monument came to him and he deciphered it during a sleepless night.' Palin explains, quite seriously, that he thereby 'thought to avoid the systematic errors that can arise only from long reflection, or whose application can only encounter difficulties'.

Not having been able to decipher the hieroglyphic inscription on the stela, he gave instead an autograph copy that included a number of errors, and reproduced Ameilhon's Latin translation of the Greek inscription. Palin put in italics the passages he believed he had read in Egyptian. Coming after the work of Silvestre de Sacy and Åkerblad, at a time when European intellectual circles were awaiting the next steps in the effort to decipher the Rosetta Stone, Palin's attempts seemed superficial and a little ridiculous. Åkerblad wrote to Young in 1816: 'I hope your system will be more convincing than that of M. Palin, who seems not to have understood much.'[2] And Champollion wrote to his brother in 1818: ' ... this will allow you to judge the true value of the explanation given by Palin, who found the whole Greek text in the hieroglyphic part of the inscription. I have no doubt that Jomard has done the same; as for Ripault, you already know what I think of his Greek scripts and columns that are curved, because they do not curve.'[3]

Jomard, who was a member of the publication committee for the *Description de l'Égypte*, had asked Champollion to meet him so they could decipher the Egyptian alphabet together. And he was mortified when Champollion destroyed his theories on the antiquity of the Dandarah zodiac,[4] which he had thought went back as far as 15,000 years, an estimate that he later revised to 12,000 years.

The English contribution was J. von Hammer-Purgstall's book *Alphabets and Hieroglyphic Characters Explained*, published in London in 1806. For his part, the director of the Musée des Monuments français, Alexandre Lenoir,[5] offered the public a work in four volumes, published from 1809 to 1821. 'The goal of this work,' the author explained, 'is to show, by the celestial sphere, that the mysteries and ancient sacred allegories are only a faithful translation of natural phenomena.' Lenoir enjoyed the Empress's favour, but he was a century or two behind the times. James Bailey[6] (in England) and Pierre Lacour[7] (in France) also had a go at the problem. All of these writers remained oddly impervious to contemporary advances in science.

Between the two champions

The polemical debate arising from the rivalry between Young and Champollion thus cannot be explained by patriotic sensitivity alone. It was inflated by the passions unleashed by the mirage of decipherment in all areas of European society, and nourished by the individual pretensions, acknowledged or not, of many of those involved. While Silvestre de Sacy arbitrated the debate in a tendentious manner, having failed to become the central figure himself, and Jomard was consumed with envy for the same reason, all kinds of people, often less well prepared than they, entered the arena. They took sides with one of the two champions, claiming to judge them and even to outdo them.

Naïve pamphlets that deliberately ignored the decisive contributions made by the *Lettre à M. Dacier* and the *Précis du système hiéroglyphique des anciens Égyptiens* continued to be published in great numbers after 1824. Champollion was therefore obliged constantly to defend his discoveries against incompetent attacks: 'So you see me, Monsieur, deprived by the highest authority of any right of property regarding the discovery of the alphabet and the hieroglyphic system; European scholars were mistaken in wishing to credit me with them, and all it will take to set common opinion right is M. Lanci's assertion to the contrary. All the same, being willing for the nonce to consider me as a sort of *titular usufructuary* of the hieroglyphic alphabet, my severe corrector magisterially proposes a major improvement that I should make, in view of the fact that in his opinion I have not very precisely determined the sound represented by some characters ...'[8]

Other attacks made by professors at foreign universities were particularly virulent, such as those of Heinrich Julius Kaproth of the University of Berlin,[9] and Gustav Seyffarth of the University of Leipzig. These two authors, Champollion wrote, 'are the willing victims of illusions', and their system, 'like

Kircher's, is not based on any series of positive facts, but only on assertions or purely personal ways of seeing things'.[10] He is annoyed particularly by those who 'vaguely claim that we still do not have any positive knowledge regarding the Egyptians' graphic system'. For example, the introduction written in 1827 by Charles Yorke and Colonel Martin Leake (members of the Royal Society of Literature in London and several other scholarly societies) for their *Egyptian Monuments in the British Museum* contained a certain number of pearls of this kind: 'Although one cannot define precisely either the degree or the nature of the phonetic power (that is, to express sound) possessed by these Egyptian hieroglyphs, it cannot be denied that they have it up to a certain point.' Or again: 'A knowledge of the Coptic language appears to be one of the most necessary things to attain this end; but scholars have made little effort to learn it.'

Among the countless authors who claimed to have deciphered the hieroglyphs, a few more positive voices made themselves heard above this chorus of scepticism. Henry Salt's, the English consul general in Egypt and great connoisseur for instance.[11] His analysis was all the more interesting because he had at hand all sorts of monuments that allowed him to back up his arguments. In France, one of the finest tributes to Champollion was made by a former detractor, Jean Antoine Letronne, who dedicated to him the publication of the Greek inscription on the Rosetta Stone.

For his part, the great German linguist Alexander von Humboldt wrote: 'I have arrived, after long study of Champollion's works, at the profound conviction that it is to him alone that this splendid discovery is due. No one can refuse him the merit of having been the first to affirm and prove that most of the hieroglyphic script is alphabetic, and while others have found a few phonetic signs, it is none the less clear that they would never even have succeeded in deciphering a significant number of proper names. Having taken the wrong path from the outset, they apparently did not devote themselves with sufficient patience to the study of the hieroglyphs, limiting themselves far too exclusively to the Rosetta inscription.'[12] Need we add that Champollion, unlike others who were seeking to decipher the inscription, had a profound knowledge of Egypt and a passionate love for the country?

The intellectual adventure that led to the decipherment of the hieroglyph lasted about thirty years. It was a collective adventure, even if the notion of teamwork had not yet become customary: whatever their value, their competence or the influence of their works, the champions of the decipherment often depended on others. It is in this spirit that we should view the rivalry between Young and Champollion.

The physicist François Arago invented probably the most convincing parable to sum up the situation. In November 1832, delivering the 'historical eulogy of Dr Thomas Young'[13] at the Académie des sciences, of which he was the permanent secretary, Arago could not avoid taking up the subject of the decipherment of the hieroglyphs: 'I hesitated a moment before confronting the passions that this question has aroused. The secretary of an academy exclusively occupied with the exact sciences might without impropriety refer this philological controversy to more competent judges ... All these scruples vanished when I considered that the interpretation of the hieroglyphs is one of the greatest discoveries of our century ...'

Arago therefore sought in Thomas Young's scientific work a situation similar to that of the decipherment of Egyptian: 'I believed I had found this example in the interferences ... Hooke had in fact said, before Thomas Young, that rays of light interfered, just as Young had assumed before Champollion that the Egyptian hieroglyphs are sometimes phonetic ... Because he did not know the composition of white light, Hooke did not have a precise idea of the nature of the interferences, just as Young for his part was mistaken in regarding the alleged syllabic or disyllabic value of hieroglyphs ... If during his lifetime Young had been given the choice of being the creator of the doctrine of interferences while leaving the hieroglyphs to Champollion, or retaining the hieroglyphs while surrendering to Hooke his ingenious theory of optics, I have no doubt that he would have hastened to acknowledge the titles of our illustrious compatriot. In addition, there would have remained to him what no one could deny him, the right to play a role in the history of the discovery of the hieroglyphs, as Kepler, Borelli, Hooke and Wren play a role in the history of the universal law of gravity.'

Champollion's legacy

There are many essays and books on Jean-François Champollion's discoveries that challenge his decipherment and propose all sorts of alternative formulas. Neither Champollion's death in 1832 nor the posthumous publication of his *Grammaire* (1836–1841) put an end to this criticism.[14] At that time, the decipherment was far from completed. It was a German, Karl Richard Lepsius, who made the next step forward.

In 1837, Lepsius published his *Lettre à M. le professeur Rosellini sur l'alphabet hiéroglyphique*.[15] He began by praising Champollion's *Grammaire*: 'a posthumous work, but one that was put in its final form by the author; we await impatiently the second part. This work, astonishing in every respect, will show the scholarly world how far the knowledge of hieroglyphs, which began by reading the name of Ptolemy on the Rosetta Stone, was advanced by its celebrated founder in the short span of eight years.'

Born in 1810 in Namburg-am-Saale, in Saxony, Lepsius attended at Sculpforta, a particularly renowned school, and went on to study Sanskrit, archaeology and art history at the universities of Leipzig, Göttingen and Berlin. After defending his doctoral thesis on 'Iguvine tables', inscriptions in Umbrian and Latin found in the town of Gubbio in Italy, he went to Paris in July 1832 to work at the Musée Charles X with the duc de Luynes, assistant director of Greek and Egyptian antiquities. He became passionately interested in ancient Egypt. After serving as secretary of the Institute of Archaeology in Rome and as professor of Egyptology at the University of Berlin, he led an expedition to Egypt and the Sudan from 1842 to 1845. Among the results of this expedition were a twelve-volume study of the Egyptian monuments[16] and the Egyptian collection in the Berlin Museum. Honours were showered on him, and from then on he spent a large part of his time in promoting the study of Egyptian, Nubian and African languages.

Among Lepsius's many works, we should mention here his study on another bilingual document, the Canopus Decree [17] discovered in Tanis, in Lower Egypt, in 1866. The analysis of this complete text put an end to the questions about the method Champollion had been the first to use. The French Egyptologist François Chabas enthusiastically declared that the Canopus Decree 'constitutes a brilliant torch that Egyptologists can use to enlighten the sceptical and indifferent. It is as if an ancient Egyptian had suddenly emerged from his windings to talk with us and to observe that we understand his language.'[18]

While Lepsius is generally regarded as Champollion's immediate successor, his subsequent heirs are countless. Once the ancient Egyptian language had been deciphered, there remained the enormous task of defining its grammar, lexicon and the epigraphy of each of the forms that it had taken over the centuries, down to its last mutation into the Coptic language. The first grammars – those by Champollion, Heinrich Karl Brugsch,[19] Victor Loret[20] and Adolf Erman[21] – did not take this evolution into account. The first to do so was Alan Henderson Gardiner's *Egyptian Grammar* (1927). This work is now partly outdated, but it remains a best-seller because reading the hieroglyphs has never been more popular among amateurs. Two centuries after the discovery of the Rosetta Stone, there are millions of 'decipherers' all over the world.

CHAPTER SIXTEEN

The magic of a script

HOW IS ancient Egyptian writing presented today to the crowds of students and amateurs that it continues to fascinate? One of the hieroglyphs' most powerful attractions resides in the contrast between the apparent simplicity of the images represented and the relative complexity of the graphic system that uses them. When one examines this script more closely, one quickly finds that it is far from easy.

A figurative script

In ancient Egypt, the word – whether pronounced, drawn or sculpted – was powerfully evocative: reading the formula for an offering was equivalent to performing the offering itself. Conversely, erasing a man's name from a stone amounted to annihilating him for ever. In the same way, dangerous animals in the Pyramid Texts were partially covered with plaster to prevent them from harming anyone.

A hieroglyph could (and this was probably its primary function) represent an object directly: ⟜ for the hand, ♈ or ⟐ for the head, 𓅞 for an ibis, or 𓀃 for a purification or 'the pure priest'.

A phonetic writing

These ideograms have not only a semantic value, but also a phonetic value. Thus the sign for hand is rendered ḏrt (djeret), that for the head in front view ḥr (her), that for the head in profile tp (tep), that for the ibis hb (heb) and that for the man pouring water on his head wᶜb (wab).★

The phonetic value was used independently of the initial content of the image, and thus served to write all sorts of other words whose meaning was unrelated to the image itself. For example, ⌑ pr (per), which represents a house seen from above and is read 'per' can be used to write the verb ⌇ pr (per), to go out. By means of such phonograms, abstract ideas can be represented graphically. Thus ♪, representing the heart and the trachea, read as nfr (nefer), renders the idea of perfection. Each sign can have one or several phonetic values. The latter are composed of one or more consonants corresponding to one or more articulations.

– *Uniliterals* are composed of a single consonant or semi-consonant and make up a pseudo-alphabet that corresponds to Champollion's 'alphabet':

𓄿 ꝫ (a), 𓇋 j (i), 𓏭 y (y), ﹍ᶜ (a), 𓅱/ᶜ w (w), 𓃀 b (b), ▯ p (p),

𓆑 f (f), 𓅓/⊏ m (m), ﹏ n (n), ⌒ r (r), 𓉻 h (h),

𓉔 ḥ (aspirate h), ⊜ ḫ (kh), ⊶ ẖ (kh),﹍/𓐍 s (s/z), ▭ š (sh),

◿ q (k), ⌒ k (k), 𓎼 g (g), ⌒ t (t), ▭ ṯ (tj), ⌒ d (d), 𓆓 ḏ (dj).

– *Biliterals* are composed of two consonants or semi-consonants:

★The letters between parentheses indicate the pronunciation, whereas those given in italics are conventional spellings used by Egyptologists the world over.

ḥ + r, ⟨owl⟩ s + 3, ⟨beetle⟩ j + n, △ m + r, etc.

– *Triliterals* are composed of three consonants or semi-consonants:

š + p + s, ⊙ ḥ + r + w, j + w + n, n + ṯ + r, etc.

Words and sentences

Ideograms and phonograms may be accompanied by signs that indicate all or some of the sounds that make them up. The offering table ⟨sign⟩ ḥtp (offering/to be satisfied) is generally written with two phonetic complements: the ⊂t and the ▯ p: ⟨sign⟩, whereas the bovid's ear ⟨sign⟩ sḏm (to hear) is usually accompanied only by the m represented by ⟨sign⟩, the owl, or by ⟨sign⟩, the rib: ⟨sign⟩.

The meaning of words can be further clarified by one or more signs called determinatives that are not read: a sitting man ⟨sign⟩ is often placed after a word designating a man, whether it is a common or a proper noun; the oil lamp ⟨sign⟩ expresses the ideas of fire, cooking, etc.; the papyrus scroll ⟨sign⟩ indicates the writing down of abstract ideas.

Taking all these elements into account, here is how a sentence on the Rosetta Stone is written. Even when they are simplified as much as possible, the explanations illustrate the extreme complexity of the Egyptian language:

rdj.t ꜥḥꜥ = f m gs.w-pr.w m r3.w-pr.w nb
'See to it that it [the stela] is set up in [all] the sanctuaries and all the temples ...'

We begin by copying the hieroglyphic text from left to right so that it follows the same order as the transliteration of the signs.

The verb ⟨hieroglyph⟩, *rdj*, 'give', takes on a particular meaning (see to it that) because it introduces an object clause. It is written using an ideogram: ⟨hieroglyph⟩ the arm with a conical loaf of bread, preceded by the phonetic complement ⟨hieroglyph⟩ *r* and accompanied by the infinitive ending ⟨hieroglyph⟩ *t*. The boat's mast ⟨hieroglyph⟩, an ideogram, represents the verb ⟨hieroglyph⟩, *ꜥḥꜥ* 'to set up'; followed by a phonetic complement ⟨hieroglyph⟩ *ꜥ* and by the determinative notated by moving legs ⟨hieroglyph⟩. Here the verb is in the passive, and its subject is the pronoun suffix ⟨hieroglyph⟩ *f* (the stela). Another sign from the pseudo-alphabet ⟨hieroglyph⟩ *m* notates the preposition 'in'. The spelling of the word 'sanctuary', ⟨hieroglyph⟩ *rꜣ.w-gs.w* is typical of the Ptolemaic period: it combines the feather with the sign for house, repeated three times in the plural. Once again, the preposition *m*, this time in the form of the rib ⟨hieroglyph⟩ introduces the complex noun ⟨hieroglyph⟩ *rꜣ.w-pr.w*. The latter is composed of the signs of the mouth ⟨hieroglyph⟩ and the house – in a Ptolemaic script that uses the form ⟨hieroglyph⟩ of the *h* – all of this in the plural, which is notated by three dashes and determined by the sign for the city ⟨hieroglyph⟩. The epithet qualifying it, 'all', is written by the basket ⟨hieroglyph⟩ *nb*, a phonogram.

The scribes' writings

The signs are not drawn or sculpted one after the other or assembled in just any way. The scribes arranged them in lines or columns, harmoniously, according to the blank spaces, starting from the left as well as from the right. Figures of men or animals faced in the direction opposite to that in which they were read; they generally faced towards the beginning of the text. When hieroglyphic inscriptions were introduced as legends for scenes, the signs were turned in the same direction as the persons concerned, whether these were men or gods. The writing was simultaneously governed by very strict rules and capable of all kinds of combinations, which allowed painters and sculptors to respect the texts to be represented while adapting them to the available surfaces.

The drawing of hieroglyphic signs was a long and meticulous process. It required a special skill and a great deal of time. Thus the scribes used a cursive script for administrative documents, correspondence, literary, magical or religious texts, mathematics and medical writings. This script, which is called 'hieratic', is a graphic simplification of hieroglyphic signs. It was always written from right to left. The most ancient hieratic texts currently known are the Gebelein papyri, the account books of a village in Upper Egypt, the archives of the royal funerary temples in Abusir and the letters from Elephantine. They go back to the end of the Fourth Dynasty and to the Fifth Dynasty. The form of the hieratic signs evolved in the course of Egyptian history, and varied depending on the handwriting of the different scribes, which it is sometimes possible to identify.

The funerary texts of the Middle and New Kingdoms – the *Coffin Texts* and the *Book of the Dead* – were often painted in columns in a cursive script intermediary between hieroglyphs and hieratic. In the late period, when hieratic script was no longer used in administration, it continued to be used in religious, magical and literary texts. From the beginning of the first millennium, however, the administration functioned autonomously in the north and the south parts of the country. Whereas in Upper Egypt the scribes employed a cursive script derived directly from hieratic, the so-called 'abnormal hieratic', the administration in Lower Egypt, which was more powerful, used a different cursive script, the 'demotic', which soon became prevalent throughout the country.

The papyrus rolls that served as books were preserved in archives, libraries and private houses, but they were found especially in temples and tombs, where the dead took their reading with them for eternity. Scribes and apprentice scribes also used bits of limestone – chips left behind by quarry workers and sculptors – and broken pots to copy out all manner of texts, both documentary and literary: the *ostraca*. Some of these recorded the everyday management of societies, while others reproduced extracts from novels, tales or prayers. During the first century BCE, when Egypt was occupied by a foreign power, administrative and juridical texts were written sometimes in the language of the occupying power (Aramaic, then Greek), and sometimes in Egyptian (demotic, then Coptic).

From the age of the gods to the end of paganism

While tradition attributes the invention of writing to the god Thoth, the most ancient hieroglyphic signs go back to the age of the chiefdoms that existed for several centuries before the unification of Egypt; they were found on the tablets that were deposited in the princely tombs in Abydos, and in them the names of institutions were already mentioned. Writings from the same period found in Mesopotamia reflected a significantly less developed image of the corresponding societies in that region. But this image may be modified by new discoveries.

The most ancient stages in the development of the Egyptian script are still difficult to reconstitute, and the earliest extant hieroglyphs, which are sometimes awkwardly inscribed, often remain incomprehensible to us. In contrast to the script, which did not change much before the Ptolemaic period, the lexicon and grammar developed considerably, to the point that an Egyptian from the Old Kingdom and another from the New Kingdom, who lived more than a millennium apart, would have had as much difficulty in understanding each other as we would have in understanding someone from the early Middle Ages. Old Egyptian, Middle Egyptian and Late Egyptian, the three main stages in the development of the language, belong to ages that differ in many respects. Middle Egyptian, which is particularly rich in literary works, is considered as the classical stage of the language, whereas Late Egyptian, which, beginning in the reign of Akhenaten, consolidated the language as it had already been spoken for several centuries, is recognizable even in Coptic.

From the fourth century CE onwards, each of Egypt's great temples developed a complex system of writing. This considerably increased the quantity of hieroglyphic signs inscribed on walls – several thousand, in comparison to 700 earlier – and the values attributed to these signs (as many as eight or nine per sign). Graphic play, already prized in earlier periods, became the rule, transforming writing and reading inscriptions into an intellectual exercise at a time when the use of hieroglyphics was limited to an erudite élite.

By prohibiting the practice of pagan cults, the Byzantine emperors, put a definitive end to the history of this extraordinary writing, the last extant example of which dates from 394 CE. The temple at Philae was the last to be closed, in 551 CE. But in the interim, Egyptian had found in Coptic a new form of alphabetical expression that was better adapted to the practices of the time.

Coptic

Retaining all the grammatical principles of Late Egyptian and most of the traditional Egyptian lexicon, Coptic was written with the Greek alphabet, to which it added seven letters borrowed from demotic.

This script, which originated during the third century CE, was used initially to notate the translation of books of the Old Testament and later that of Gospels. It was soon more widely adopted by Egyptian Christians, and was also used in everyday life for letters, accounts and so on. Thus, abandoning the old gods to serve the new faith, Egyptian found a way of surviving.

Alphabet copte.

À gauche, les sept lettres supplémentaires à l'alphabet grec; au centre, leur équivalent en démotique, dont ils sont tirés; à droite, leur transcription hiéroglyphique (d'après J. Vergote, Grammaire copte, Louvain, 1973).

Coptic alphabet. (Right column): At left, the seven letters supplementing the Greek alphabet; centre, their equivalent in demotic, from which they are derived; right, their hieroglyphic transcription (after J. Vergote, Grammaire copte, Louvain, 1973).

Research, in the age of software

Independently of their ideographic or phonetic identity, the form of the signs – whether hieroglyphic, hieratic or demotic – is worth studying case by case. In fact, depending on the period of the document in question, and sometimes depending on the material support (stone, papyrus or ostracon) and the personality and skill of the draughtsman, engraver or sculptor, a single character may vary considerably. These variations can be classified in tables that make it possible to situate them in time and space.

This kind of research, indispensable for hieratic and demotic – which are more or less easy to read, depending on the scribe – is still embryonic so far as hieroglyphs are concerned. Monuments using hieroglyphs are far more numerous, making the task almost impossible. While the identification of the characters is in general not very difficult, we often do not know at what time a given sign was first attested. We would also like to be able to date documents with rare graphic forms, or at least to be able to verify that these were or were not known.

The celebrations connected with the hundred-and-fiftieth anniversary of the *Lettre à M. Dacier*, in 1972, offered an opportunity to assess the research conducted and the knowledge acquired regarding the Egyptian language since 1822.[1] This research and knowledge have continued to make significant progress, notably through the introduction of linguistic methods. Alongside the conventional interpretation of hieroglyphic, hieratic and demotic signs, studies on phonetics seek to determine more precisely the actual pronunciation of words, which varied depending on the period and the region, as is shown by the dialectological studies that can be conducted essentially on Coptic.

Lexicography still has much to discover. Many questions persist regarding the translation of texts from all periods, and each new text edited contributes its bit of obscure vocabulary. Researchers working individually or in teams – the latter are sometimes international – are undertaking the study of specific vocabularies, and updating existing dictionaries or conceiving new ones.

In 1972, Jacques Jean Clère observed: 'While the research carried out over the past decades has considerably increased our knowledge of the grammar of Middle Egyptian, we are still far from having mastered all its rules or grasped all its sub-tleties. The particularly weak point is still the verb system, and this is not surprising, since this system is based both on variations in vocalism and on the (supposed) presence of geminate consonants characterizing certain forms, two phonetic peculiarities that are completely absent in hieroglyphic writing. It is therefore not surprising that it is especially regarding the verb system that grammarians have still not achieved agreement.'

These debates among specialists, which are becoming increasingly technical, have not diminished the magical powers of the hieroglyph. While no one any longer fears that a horned viper, leaving its function as a pronoun suffix, might suddenly come alive and strike an imprudent reader, the fascination exercised by these signs continues to grow. In addition to the mystery that used to shroud them and which for many people they still have, even if we can now understand them, there is a playful or aesthetic pleasure to be had from them. In an age when software for producing hieroglyphs is being developed and used all over the world, Champollion's *Egyptian Grammar*, even though today its value is only bibliographical and senti-mental, still makes generations of amateurs dream. With a certain regret, however – the hieroglyphs have already been deciphered.

CHAPTER SEVENTEEN

The fate of a stone

NO ONE considers it an artistic masterpiece. This broken stela covered with inscriptions cuts a poor figure when compared to the many treasures of ancient Egypt. And God knows the British Museum has some! But no matter: the Rosetta Stone is a star object, a monument that no visitor to the museum in London can afford to miss.

In Hall no. 25, on the ground floor, near the main entrance, the Stone was for a long time enclosed in a wooden frame and protected by glass. The frame was finally removed. Then in 1980, at the request of the public, the glass was also removed, allowing visitors to touch 'the stone with three inscriptions' as one touches a relic. This liberal attitude did not please everyone: the British Museum's Egyptian department was bombarded with letters claiming that this precious object was being spoilt, and in particular that the white of its letters was being worn away. In the mid-1980s, it was decided to protect the stela by installing a rope barrier; in order to touch the stone, one had to lean far over, and almost no one tried it ...

Since 1988, the Rosetta Stone no longer dominates the gallery from its central position. It has been moved a few metres away: on its granite and metal base, it is now in a sort of alcove, protected by a rope. Untouchable.

The move provided an opportunity to clean the Stone. This belated operation brought out a pink vein in its upper left part. The stela is not black, as had been previously thought, but dark grey. Moreover, it is not basalt, but granite. It took almost two hundred years for this to be noticed. In the museum's laboratory, a tiny sample taken from the back of the monument was examined under a microscope, revealing that it was in fact a granitoid stone rich in quartz and containing feldspar and mica. In speaking of a 'black granite stone' Napoleon's officers and scientists were not so far from the truth.

Originally, the letters inscribed on the stela bore only a few traces of red pigment. They were filled with white chalk when the Stone was installed in the British Museum – and retouched at the beginning of the 1980s – to make the inscriptions more visible. As for the black covering the Stone, it resulted, according the museum's specialists, from 'the application of wax intended to preserve the surface, but which absorbed the dust in the London atmosphere for two centuries'.

Will the new colours be adopted by the makers of souvenirs and trinkets? The British Museum's shop offers visitors countless ways of taking a bit of the Stone with them – posters, T-shirts, scarves, ties, mugs, pencil-sharpeners, mouse pads, puzzles – not to mention plastic resin replicas in various sizes. The black might be replaced by grey, and a pink vein could even be put into all the copies. But to go as far as to do away with the white letters, well ...

Today, the famous 'Captured in Egypt' is hardly visible. The wax seems to have managed to flow over the side, as if to erase this relic from the battles of another age. Moreover, in July 1999 the museum took advantage of the two-hundredth anniversary of the discovery of the Rosetta Stone to redo its information panels. The old ones, which were very biased, detailed at length the merits of Thomas Young, his intuitions and his discoveries, while Jean-François Champollion appeared in second place. Champollion was accorded the title of 'father of the decipherment of the hieroglyphs' in spite of his initial errors and his refusal to recognize that Young's studies antedated his own.

A single journey to Paris

In two hundred years, the Rosetta Stone has left the British Museum only once. And it may never leave again. French Egyptologists have repeatedly asked that it be loaned to them, but they have encountered a categorical refusal: this stela will not leave London.

Another attempt was made in 1972, on the occasion of the hundred-and-fiftieth anniversary of the *Lettre à M. Dacier*. Jean Leclant, then president of the French Society of Egyptology, took advantage of the Duke of Edinburgh's visit to Paris to urge him to back the request. At the Invalides, during an equestrian parade, in pouring rain, he approached the prince, who looked at him in amazement ...

The Louvre museum also sent an official request to the head of the British Museum's Egyptian department, I. E. S. Edwards, who was very cooperative, and said that the request would be submitted to the museum's trustees. But a few weeks later he wrote regretfully that the trustees had voted unanimously against the transfer.

This did not surprise the head curator of the Louvre's Egyptian department, Jacques Vandier, who had gone through the motions of making the request without expecting it to be granted. However, his main colleague, Christiane Desroches-Noblecourt, was astonished: 'What were they afraid we would do to a stone as solid as that one? That we would keep it? Give it back to the Egyptians? I neither understand it nor resign myself to it, but all parallel requests made at the time, including the active intervention of the director-general of Unesco, René Maheu, remained fruitless.'[1]

Desroches-Noblecourt's surprise was all the greater because she had recently urged the Egyptian government to grant the British Museum's request for the loan of a precious statue of Tutankhamen. As a result, the statue, which belonged to the Cairo Museum and had been restored by the French, was sent to London to be part of the exhibit celebrating the fiftieth anniversary of the discovery, in 1922, of the treasure in Tutankhamen's tomb – a one hundred per cent British discovery made by the Egyptologist Howard Carter, sponsored by his compatriot the Earl of Carnarvon.

At the party held to celebrate the opening of the London exhibit, Christiane Desroches-Noblecourt learned that the request that the Rosetta Stone be lent had never been submitted to the British Museum's trustees. Furious, she demanded an explanation. Queen Elizabeth, who was present at the party, was then informed of the French request. The following day, Her Majesty granted permission for the stela to travel to Paris for a month.

In October, the Rosetta Stone was transported to the French capital, accompanied by Harry James, a curator at the British Museum. It arrived, with its base and protective glass, after crossing the Channel on a car-ferry. It was installed at the Louvre, in the Henri IV gallery, which had been completely renovated, in front of the bas-relief representing Seti I and the goddess Hathor. Many schoolchildren, guided by their teachers, came to see it, but there were no crowds, and the press paid the event little attention. It has to be said that the Louvre's administrators avoided any hype in order not to upset the English. A single postcard was created for the occasion.

Temporarily, visitors to the British Museum had to make do with a cast replacement. *The Times* published an article by the head curator of the Egyptian department entitled 'Tutankhamen's debt to the Rosetta Stone'.[2] His goal was not to discuss the loan of the stela, but rather – and this is another sign of the times – to emphasize all that visitors to the London exhibit owed to Champollion, without whom we would understand nothing about the vestiges of ancient Egypt.

The Rosetta Stone returned to London without a hitch a month later. This historic visit made fewer waves on both sides of the Channel than had been expected. After one hundred and seventy years, the French-English polemic seems to have come to an end, with Tutankhamen's help.

In 1991, Figeac, Champollion's native city, installed a giant replica of the Rosetta Stone. This work, by the American artist Joseph Kossuth, was created from a slab of black granite from Zimbabwe, 11 metres long by 8.5 metres wide. A photographic process made it possible to reproduce the stela in its smallest details. Kossuth's stone covers almost the whole surface of a small pedestrian square in the heart of the old city. Inserted into the pavement, it follows the natural slope of the land: its three steps, each bearing an inscription, mark the passage from one script to another. It can be admired from a small 'Egyptian-style' garden perched on a viewpoint where papyrus, tamarisks and various aromatic or medicinal plants are growing. But one can also walk over the engraved slab or sit on it and dream. This square is appropriately called la place des Écritures.

The Egyptians' bitterness

Since it did not have the original, the Cairo Museum also created a replica of the Rosetta Stone. It is located on the right, in the entrance hall, immediately after the security gate.

Another replica is exhibited 200 kilometres away, on the site where the Rosetta Stone was discovered: the ex-Fort Julien, which has long since recovered its old name of Borg Rashid, and whose renovation in 1985 turned it into virtually a new building. Here, 'Rosetta' doesn't mean anything to anyone. The city bears the more virile name of Rashid. It is visited by Egyptians as a site of Muslim archaeology: people go there to admire its mosques and ancient houses built of red and black bricks, corbelled over the streets. All around, the countryside retains its character rather well. The 'city of a thousand palms' proudly recalls its victorious resistance to the British invasion of 1807, but seems hardly to remember that it also sheltered a famous stela. Or perhaps it pretends to forget, knowing that the 'stone with three inscriptions' will probably never return to the banks of the Nile.

The possibility of such a return is a subject regularly discussed. Every time a major Egyptian exhibit is organized abroad, some newspaper in Cairo demands, adopting a polemical tone, 'the restitution of parts of our national heritage that have been stolen from us'. The bust of Nefertiti (in the Berlin Museum), a fragment of the Sphinx's beard (in the British Museum), and, of course, the Rosetta Stone, are always mentioned. The most intransigent writers even demand the return of monuments given in the nineteenth century to various European countries by Mohammed Ali and his successors. These gifts were illegal, they claim, because Egyptian rulers did not have the right to give away the national heritage.

In reality, no serious person would ask that the hundreds of thousands of Egyptian monuments in European and American museums be returned to Egypt. Egypt wouldn't know where to put them. Its own museums are collapsing under the weight of treasures they lack the space to exhibit. More positively, Egyptian authorities know that the Louvre, the British Museum, New York's Metropolitan Museum and their equivalents in Berlin and Turin provide an excellent introduction to the land of the pharaohs, and marvellous publicity for the valley of the Nile. Wisdom suggests that the gifts, purchases and even thefts of earlier times should not be challenged now. History cannot be rewritten. But how can one prevent the question from resurfacing regularly and focusing on a piece as symbolic as the Rosetta Stone?

Egyptians have seen two European powers battling for this monument on their soil. At the beginning of the nineteenth century, that mattered little: the descendants of the pharaohs were the last to take an interest in pharaonic relics. This is no longer true today, when Egyptians are proud of this heritage and aware of its economic importance. In a meaningful way, the country is experiencing a wave of architectural Egyptomania: to realize this, one has only to visit the new cities, such as the one known as '6 October'. Every year, the universities train hundreds of new Egyptologists, and to these we must add the tourist guides. If these Egyptologists are still not as advanced as their foreign counterparts, they have the great advantage of knowing the country from the inside, and thus of being able to explore its past with a special kind of insight.

The two-hundredth anniversary of the discovery of the Rosetta Stone could hardly be an occasion for great festivities in Egypt. First of all, because 'the most important ancient monument is hundreds of kilometres away from the nation's territory', as Dr Ali Hassan, who was then director of the Antiquities Service, pointed out.[3] And secondly, because the discovery took place during the French expedition, another, even more delicate subject of polemics. In order to celebrate the decipherment of the hieroglyphics, wasn't it simpler to wait for the centenary of the *Lettre à M. Dacier*, in ... 2022?

The symbol of the decipherment

Champollion's discovery is sometimes presented as 'the encounter between a man and a stone'. This is a fine formula, but it goes too far in two respects: on one hand, Champollion never saw the famous stela, which he knew only through more or less reliable copies, and on the other, the Rosetta Stone was only one of the elements that allowed him to understand the writing of ancient Egypt. In this colossal achievement, the crucial factor was his knowledge of Near Eastern languages, and particularly Coptic.

All the same, the role of the Rosetta Stone should not be underestimated. It was both a formidable challenge and a starting point. Champollion examined it over and over again before turning to other documents. And he profited from the work of Silvestre de Sacy, Åkerblad and Young, who had worked essentially on the stela. The decipherment of the hieroglyphs was not the work of one man alone.

Would the hieroglyphs have been deciphered without the Rosetta Stone? No doubt, but it would have taken longer. The discovery in 1866 of an intact bilingual stela that included another decree – that of Canopus – could have made it possible. One must be wary of such claims, however. What is more important, a bilingual monument or the hard work, competence and exceptional gifts of a man like Champollion?

The Rosetta Stone is inseparable from this unprecedented intellectual adventure that challenged several extraordinary figures for a quarter of a century. It will always remain the symbol of decipherment, the brilliant materialization of a dream that became a reality.

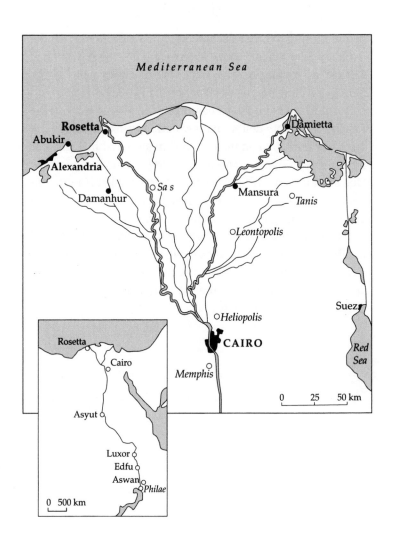

The Memphis Decree

In what order were the three texts on the Rosetta Stone inscribed? According to Wilhelm Spiegelberg, a German Egyptologist and expert on demotic, the process may have gone through a number of stages: (1) a first draft in demotic, registering the synod's decisions; (2) the official text drawn up in Greek by a limited committee; (3) the final demotic translation, in which the influence of the word order of the Greek is obvious; (4) the final version in hieroglyphs, which is the least reliable.[1]

More recently, Philippe Derchain has arrived at the conclusion that 'there was no demotic or Greek original; the two versions must have been composed simultaneously and rely on one another, depending on the origin of the subject matter to be formulated. On the other hand, the royal titulature is complete only in the hieroglyphic version, and it is the only element that seems to have been imposed on the two other versions, which more or less translate it.'[2]

The demotic text of the Memphis Decree on the Rosetta Stone

A translation by R. S. Simpson

[Year 9, Xandikos day 4], which is equivalent to the Egyptian month, second month of Peret, day 18 of the King 'The Youth who has appeared as King in the place of his Father', the Lord of the Uraei 'Whose might is great, who has established Egypt, causing it to prosper, whose heart is beneficial before the gods', (the One) Who is over his Enemy 'Who has caused the life of the people to prosper, the Lord of the Years of Jubilee like Ptah-Tenen, King like Pre', [the King of the Upper Districts and] the Lower Districts 'The Son of the Father-loving Gods, whom Ptah has chosen, to whom Pre has given victory, the Living Image of Amun', the Son of Pre 'Ptolemy, living for ever, beloved of Ptah, the Manifest God whose excellence is fine', son of Ptolemy and Arsinoe, the Father-loving Gods, (and) the Priest of Alexander and the Saviour Gods and [the Brother-and-Sister Gods and the] Beneficent [Gods] and the Father-loving Gods and King Ptolemy, the Manifest God whose excellence is fine, Aetos son of Aetos; while Pyrrha daughter of Philinos was Prize-bearer before Berenice the Beneficent, while Areia daughter of Diogenes was [Basket]-bearer [before Arsi] know the Brother-loving, and while Eirene daughter of Ptolemy was Priestess of Arsinoe the Father-loving: on this day, a decree of the mr-sn priests and the ḥm-nṯr priests, and the priests who enter the sanctuary to perform clothing rituals for the gods, and the scribes of the devine book and the scribes of the House of Life, and the other priests who have come from the temples of Egypt [to Memphis on] the festival of the Reception of the Rulership by King Ptolemy, living for ever, beloved of Ptah, the Manifest God whose excellence is fine, from his father, who have assembled in the temple of Memphis, and who have said:

Whereas King Ptolemy, living for ever, the Manifest God whose excellence is fine, son of King Ptolemy [and Queen] Arsinoe, the Father-loving Gods, is wont to do many favours for the temples of Egypt and for all those who are subject to his kingship, he being a god, the son of a god and a goddess, and being like Horus son of Isis and Osiris, who protects his father Osiris, and his heart being beneficent concerning the gods, since he has given much money and much grain to the temples of Egypt, [he having undertaken great expenses] in order to create peace in Egypt and to establish the temples, and having rewarded all the forces that are subject to his rulership; and of the revenues and taxes that were in force in Egypt he had reduced some or(?) had renounced them completely, in order to cause the army and all the other people to be prosperous in his time as [king; the arrear]s which were due to the King from the people who are in Egypt and all those who are subject to his kingship, and (which) amounted to a large total, he renounced; the people who were in prison and those against whom there had been charges for a long time, he released; he ordered concerning the endowments of the gods, and the money and the grain that are given as allowances to their [temples] each year, and the shares that belong to the gods from the vineyards, the orchards, and all the rest of the property which they possessed under his father, that they should remain in their possession; moreover, he ordered concerning the priests that they should not pay their tax on becoming priests above what they used to pay up to Year 1 under his father; he released the people [who hold] the offices of the temples from the voyage they used to make to the Residence of Alexander each year; he ordered that no rower should be impressed into service; he renounced the two-thirds share of the fine linen that used to be made in the temples for the Treasury, he bringing into its [correct] state everything that had abandoned its (proper) condition for a long time, and taking all care to have done in a correct manner what is customarily done for the gods, likewise causing justice to be done for the people in accordance with what Thoth the Twice-great did; moreover, he ordered concerning those who will return from the fighting men and the rest of the people who had gone astray (lit. been on other ways) in the disturbance that had occurred in Egypt that [they] should [be returned] to their homes, and their possessions should be restored to them; and he took all care to send (foot) soldiers, horsemen, and ships against those who came by the shore and by the sea to make an attack on Egypt; he spent a great amount in money and grain against these (enemies), in order to ensure that the temples and the people who were in Egypt should be secure; he went to the fortress of Sk3n [which had] been fortified by the rebels with all kinds of work, there being much gear and all kinds of equipment within it; he enclosed that fortress with a wall and a dyke(?) around (lit. outside) it, because of the rebels who were inside it, who had already done much harm to Egypt, and abandoned the way of the commands of the King and the commands [of the god]s; he caused the canals which supplied water to that fortress to be dammed off, although the previous kings could not have done likewise, and much money was expended on them; he assigned a force of footsoldiers and horsemen to the mouths of those canals, in order to watch over them and to protect them, because of the [rising] of the water, which was great in Year 8, while those canals supply water to much land and are very deep; the King took that fortress by storm in a short time; he overcame the rebels who were within it, and slaughtered them in accordance with what Pre and Horus son of Isis did to those who had rebelled against them in those places in the Beginning; (as for) the rebels who had gathered armies and led them to disturb the nomes, harming the temples and abandoning the way of the King and his father, the gods let him overcome them at Memphis during the festival of the Reception of the Rulership which he did from his father, and he had them slain on the wood; he remitted the arrears that were due

to the King from the temples up to Year 9, and amounted to a
large total of money and grain; likewise the value of the fine
linen that was due from the temples from what is made for the
Treasury, and the verification fees(?) of what had been made up
to that time; moreover, he ordered concerning the artaba of
wheat per aroura of land, which used to be collected from the
fields of the endowment, and likewise for the wine per aroura
of land from the vineyards of the gods' endowments: he renounced them; he did many favours for Apis and Mnevis, and
the other sacred animals that are honoured in Egypt, more
than what whose who were before him used to do, he being devoted to their affairs at all times, and giving what is required
for their burials, although it is great and splendid, and provid-
ing what is dedicated(?) in their temples when festivals are celebrated and burnt offerings made before them, and the rest of
the things which it is fitting to do; the honours which are due
to the temples and the other honours of Egypt he caused to be
established in their (proper) condition in accordance with the
law; he gave much gold, silver, grain, and other items for the
Place of Apis; he had it adorned with new work as very fine
work; he had new temples, sanctuaries, and altars set up for
the gods, and caused others to assume their (proper) condition, he having the heart of a beneficent god concerning the
gods and enquiring after the honours of the temples, in order
to renew them in his time as king in the manner that is fitting;
and the gods have given him in return for these things
strength, victory, success(?), prosperity, health, and all the (sic)
other favours, his kingship being established under him and
his descendants for ever:

With good fortune! It has seemed fitting to the priests of
all the temples of Egypt, as to the honours which are due to
King Ptolemy, living for ever, the Manifest God whose excellence is fine, in the temples, and those which are due to the
Father-loving Gods, who brought him into being, and those

which are due to the Beneficent Gods, who brought into being
those who brought him into being, and those which are due to
the Brother-and-Sister Gods, who brought into being those
who brought them into being, and those which are due to the
Saviour Gods, the Ancestors of his ancestors, to increase
them; and that a statue should be set up for King Ptolemy, living for ever, the Manifest God whose excellence is fine – which
should be called 'Ptolemy who has protected the Bright Land',
the meaning of which is 'Ptolemy who has preserved Egypt' –
together with a statue for the local god, giving him a scimitar
of victory, in each temple, in the public part of the temple, they
being made in the manner of Egyptian work; and the priests
should pay service to the statues in each temple three times a
day, and they should lay down sacred objects before them and
do for them the rest of the things that it is normal to do, in accordance with what is done for the other gods on the festivals,
the processions, and the named (holi)days; and there should
be produced a cult image for King Ptolemy, the Manifest God
whose excellence is fine, son of Ptolemy and Queen Arsinoe,
the Father-loving Gods, together with the (sic) shrine in each
temple, and it should be installed in the sanctuary with the
other shrines; and when the great festivals occur, on which the
gods are taken in procession, the shrine of the Manifest God
whose excellence is fine should be taken in procession with
them; and in order that the shrine may be recognized, now and
in the rest of the times that are to come, ten royal diadems of
gold should be added – there being one uraeus on them each,
like what is normally done for the gold diadems – on top of the
shrine, instead of the uraei that are upon the rest of the
shrines; and the double crown should be in the centre of the diadems, because it is the one with which the King was crowned
in the temple of Memphis, when there was being done for him
what is normally done at the Reception of the Rulership; and
there should be placed on the upper side of (the) square(?)
which is outside the diadems, and opposite the gold diadem

that is described above, a papyrus plant and a 'sedge' plant;
and a uraeus should be placed on a basket with a 'sedge' under
it on the right of the side on top of the shrine, and a uraeus
with a basket under it should be placed on a papyrus on the
left, the meaning of which is 'The King who has illumined
Upper and Lower Egypt'; and whereas fourth month of Shemu,
last day, on which is held the birthday of the King, has been
established already as a procession festival in the temples, likewise second month of Peret, day 17, on which are performed
for him the ceremonies of the Reception of the Rulership – the
beginning of the good things that have happened to everyone:
the birth of the King, living for ever, and his reception of the
rulership – let these days, the 17th and the last, become festivals each month in all the temples of Egypt; and there should
be performed burnt offerings, libations, and the rest of the
things that are normally done on the other festivals, on both
festivals each month; and what is offered in sacrifice(?) should
be distributed as a surplus(?) to the people who serve in the
temple; and a procession festival should be held in the temples
and the whole of Egypt for King Ptolemy, living for ever, the
Manifest God whose excellence is fine, each year, from first
month of Akhet, day 1, for five days, with garlands being worn,
burnt offerings and libations being performed, and the rest of
the things that it is fitting to do; and the priests who are in each
of the temples of Egypt should be called 'The Priests of the
Manifest God whose excellence is fine' in addition to the other
priestly titles, and they should write it on every document, and
they should write the priesthood of the Manifest God whose
excellence is fine on their rings and they should engrave it on
them; and it should be made possible for the private persons
also who will (so) wish, to produce the likeness of the shrine of
the Manifest God whose excellence is fine, which is (discussed) above, and to keep it in their homes and hold the festivals and the processions which are described above, each year,
so that it may become known that the inhabitants of Egypt pay

honour to the Manifest God whose excellence is fine in accordance with what is normally done;

And the decree should be written on a stela of hard stone, in sacred writing, document writing, and Greek writing, and it should be set up in the first-class temples, the second-class temples and the third-class temples, next to the statue of the King, living for ever.

[Revised version from R. S. Simpson, *Demotic Grammar in the Ptolemaic Sacerdotal Decrees* (Oxford, 1996), pp. 258–71, as reproduced in Richard Parkinson, *Cracking Codes: the Rosetta Stone and decipherment* (London, 1999). Copyright: The Griffith Institute. Ashmolean Museum, Oxford, by whose permission it is reproduced.]

Other bilingual stelae

'FOR AN Egyptian antiquarian, the discovery of the missing part of the Rosetta Stone would be worth its weight in diamonds,' Thomas Young wrote to William Bankes on 10 February 1815. This upper part of the stone (which must have been topped with an engraved arch, like other stelae of the same type) has never been found. On the other hand, several other versions of the Memphis Decree, some complete and some incomplete, have been discovered:

- A basalt stela with an arched top (1.20 metres by 0.77 metres, 0.22 metres thick), whose lower part is broken, was purchased in 1923 by the French Egyptologist Henri Gauthier in Nub-Taha, near Tell-el-Yahudieh (Leontopolis), in the east delta. Today, it is in the Alexandria Museum (no. 21352). The stela had been used as an oil press. Only the Greek text of the decree is engraved, in incomplete form, on the sides of the stela.[1]

- Three fragments of a sandstone stela were found in 1907 by Jean Clédat and Clermont-Ganneau during their excavations on Elephantine. They bear parts of inscriptions in hieroglyphic, demotic and Greek, respectively, and are now in the Louvre. By chance, one of these fragments corresponds to the part of the text on the Rosetta Stone that has an increasingly large lacuna at the end of each line, and this has made it possible to check the restitutions that have been proposed.[2]

- A complete sandstone stela, including the only hieroglyphic version of the Memphis Decree, was purchased by the Bulak Museum (Cairo) in December 1884, in El-Noberieh, near Damanhur (no. 5576). It probably came from the nearby temple of Naukratis. But the very nature of the errors in the inscription – words cut off, suffixes forgotten – shows that it is a copy made from an original by a second-rate stone-cutter who did not understand the meaning of what he was engraving.[3] Despite the defects of this text, the monument has the advantage of giving us a general idea of what the various copies of the stone looked like. As on the majority of Egyptian stelae, the arch is occupied by a double scene of sacrificial offerings.

Another decree, dating from the twenty-first year of the reign of Ptolemy V Epiphanes, is engraved on the east wall of the *pronaos* or vestibule of the *mammisi* of the temple of Isis in Philae. Its purpose was to extend to Queen Cleopatra the honours previously rendered only to the king. But the Greek text is lacking, and the double Egyptian inscription (in hieroglyphics and demotic) was later covered over by reliefs of Neos Dionysos.[4] This decree was reproduced by Lepsius in his *Denkmäler*, vol. IV, p. 20.

The Canopus Decree

In 1866, about forty years after the hieroglyphs were deciphered, another bilingual decree, known as the 'Canopus Decree' was found at San-el-Hagar (Tanis). Reading it made it possible to confirm in a striking manner Champollion's demonstrations and the works of his successors.

This decree was composed by the priests assembled in a synod at Canopus, a city in the delta near Alexandria, in 238 BCE, to celebrate the birthday and accession to the throne of Ptolemy III Euergetes. Therefore this document is earlier than the Memphis Decree. In it, the priests rendered homage to the king and his daughter Berenice, but it seems that the true purpose of this decree was to reform the calendar: Ptolemy III wanted to add an extra day every four years in order to put an end to a shift that threw off the seasons. However, he apparently did not succeed in convincing the clergy.[5]

The three versions of the Canopus Decree – in contrast to that of Memphis – are rigorously parallel.[6] Six copies are currently extant:

- The Table of Tanis, discovered in May 1866 by Karl Richard Lepsius, relying on information provided by a French engineer working on the Suez Canal, is complete. It is a limestone slab with hieroglyphic and Greek inscriptions on its front, whereas the demotic inscription is on its sides.
- An equally complete stela, which was in even better condition than the Table of Tanis, was found by Gaston Maspero in Kom-el-Hisn, in the delta, in 1881. In this case, the three versions – hieroglyphic, demotic and Greek – are engraved on the front of the stela.
- Two basalt fragments from the doorsill of the Kour mosque in Cairo are preserved in Paris, in the Louvre (no. C122).
- A sandstone fragment was discovered in El-Kab during excavations conducted by the Fondation égyptologique Reine-Élisabeth. It is now in the Cairo Museum, with the temporary number [see figure on p. 194F].
- A basalt fragment with a hieroglyphic inscription from Bubastis and deposited in the Port Said Museum (no. 493).[7]

- An unpublished Theban version in pink granite, including the complete hieroglyphic inscription (which is, however, erased) and the first lines of the demotic text. The Greek text was not inscribed.[8]

Thomas Young's intuitions

The results of Thomas Young's research were published in 1819 in the Supplement to the Encyclopaedia Britannica. This text, which is twenty pages long and is entitled 'Egypt', allows us to gauge, three years before the Lettre à M. Dacier, Young's contribution to the deciphering of the hieroglyphics, as well as the limits of his demonstration and the errors he committed. Here is the text of the sixth part of Young's article, which is devoted to an 'Analysis of the triple inscription from Rosetta'.

Having acquired some preliminary notions of the mythology and history, and chronology and institutions, of ancient Egypt, we may proceed to the discussion of its written language and literature, as far as they are likely to be recovered from existing monuments; and, first of all, we must inquire into the best mode of obtaining some satisfactory conclusions from the invaluable inscriptions in honour of Ptolemy Epiphanes; which contain the only authentic specimen in existence of hieroglyphical characters expressly accompanied by a translation.

The block or pillar of black basalt, found by the French in digging up some ground at Rosetta, and now placed in the British Museum, exhibits the remains of three distinct inscriptions: and the last, which is in Greek, ends with the information, that the decree, which it contains, was ordered to be engraved in three different characters, the sacred letters, the letters of the country, and the Greek. Unfortunately a considerable part of the first inscription is wanting: the beginning of

the second, and the end of the third, are also mutilated; so that
we have no precise points of coincidence from which we can
set out, in our attempts to decipher the unknown characters.
The second inscription, which it will be safest to distinguish by
the Greek name *enchorial*, signifying merely the characters 'of
the county', notwithstanding its deficiencies near the beginning, is still sufficiently perfect to allow us to compare its different parts with each other, and with the Greek, by the same
method that we should employ if it were entire. Thus, if we examine the parts corresponding, in their relative situation, to
two passages of the Greek inscription in which *Alexander* and
Alexandria occur, we soon recognize two well marked groups of
characters resembling each other, which we may therefore
consider as representing these names; a remark which was
first made by Mr de Sacy, in his Letter relating to this inscription. A small group of characters, occurring very often in almost every line, might be either some termination, or some
very common particle: it must, therefore, be reserved till it is
found in some decisive situation, after some other words have
been identified, and it will then easily be shown to mean *and*.
The next remarkable collection of characters is repeated
twenty-nine or thirty times in the enchorial inscription; and we
find nothing that occurs so often in the Greek, except the word
king, with its compounds, which is found about thirty-seven
times. A fourth assemblage of characters is found fourteen
times in the enchorial inscription, agreeing sufficiently well in
frequency with the name of *Ptolemy*, which occurs eleven times
in the Greek, and generally in passages corresponding to those
of the enchorial text in their relative situation: and, by a similar
comparison, the name of Egypt is identified, although it occurs much more frequently in the enchorial inscription than in
the Greek, which often substitutes for it country only, or omits
it entirely. Having thus obtained a sufficient number of common points of subdivision, we may next proceed to write the
Greek text over the enchorial, in such a manner that the pas-

sages ascertained may all coincide as nearly as possible; and it is obvious that the intermediate parts of each inscription will then stand very near to the corresponding passages of the other.

In this process, it will be necessary to observe that the lines of the enchorial inscription are written from right to left, as, Herodotus tells us, was the custom of the Egyptians; the division of several words and phrases plainly indicating the direction in which they are to be read. It is well known that the distinct hieroglyphical inscriptions, engraved on different monuments, differ in the direction of the corresponding characters: they always face the right or the left of the spectator according as the principal personages of the tablets, to which they belong, are looking in the one or the other direction; where, however, there are no tablets, they almost always look towards the right; and it is easily demonstrable that they must always have been read beginning from the front, and proceeding to the rear of each rank. But the Egyptians seem never to have written alternately backwards and forwards, as the most ancient Greeks occasionally did. In both cases, however, the whole of the characters thus employed were completely reversed in the two different modes of using them, as if they were seen in a glass, or printed off like the impression of a seal.

By pursuing the comparison of the inscriptions, thus arranged, we ultimately discover the signification of the greater part of the individual enchorial words; and the result of the investigation leads us to observe some slight differences in the form and order of some parts of the different inscriptions, which are indicated in the 'conjectural translation,' published in the *Archaeologia* and in the *Museum Criticum*. The degree of evidence in favour of the supposed signification of each assemblage of characters may be most conveniently appreciated, by arranging them in a lexicographical form, according to the words of the translation; the enchorial words themselves not readily admitting a similar arrangement: but the subject is not of sufficient interest for the public, to make it necessary that this little lexicon should be engraved at length.

It might naturally have been expected that the final characters of the enchorial inscription, of which the sense is thus determined with tolerable certainty, although the corresponding part of the Greek is wanting, would have immediately led us to a knowledge of the concluding phrase of the distinct hieroglyphical characters, which remains unimpaired. But the agreement between the two conclusions is by no means precise; and the difficulty can only be removed by supposing the king to be expressly named in the one, while he is only designated by his titles in the other. With this slight variation, and with the knowledge of the singular accident, that the name of Ptolemy occurs three times in a passage of the enchorial inscription, where the Greek has it but twice, we proceed to identify this name among the sacred characters, in a form sufficiently conspicuous, to have been recognized upon the most superficial examination of the inscriptions, if this total disagreement of the frequency of occurrence had not imposed the condition of a long and laborious investigation, as an indispensable requisite for the solution of so much of the enigma: this step, however, being made good, we obtain from it a tolerably correct scale for the comparative extent of the sacred characters, of which it now appears that almost half of the lines are entirely wanting, those which remain being also much mutilated. Such a scale may also be obtained, in a different manner, by marking, on a straight ruler, the places in which the most characteristic words, such as god, king, priest, and shrine occur, in the latter parts of the other inscriptions, at distances proportional to the actual distances from the end; and then trying to find corresponding characters among the hieroglyphics of the first inscription, by varying the obliquity of the ruler, so as to correspond to all possible lengths which that inscription can be supposed to have occupied, allowing always a certain latitude for the variations of the comparative lengths of the different phrases and expressions. By these steps it is not very difficult to assure ourselves, that a *shrine* and a *priest* are denoted by representations which must have been intended for pictures of objects denoted by them; and this appears to be the precise point of the investigation at which it becomes completely demonstrative, and promises a substantial foundation for further inferences. The other terms, *god* and *king*, are still more easily ascertained, from their situation near the name of Ptolemy ...

In thus comparing the enchorial with the sacred characters, we find many coincidences in their forms, by far too accurate to be compatible with the supposition that the enchorial could be of a nature purely alphabetical. It is evident, for example that the enchorial characters for a *diadem*, an *asp*, and *ever-living*, are immediately borrowed from the sacred. But this coincidence can certainly not be traced throughout the inscriptions; and it seemed natural to suppose, that alphabetical characters might be interspersed with hieroglyphics, in the same way that the astronomers and chemists of modern times have often employed arbitrary marks, as compendious expressions of the objects which were most frequently to be mentioned in their respective sciences. But no effort, however determined and persevering, had been able to discover any alphabet, which could fairly be said to render the inscription, in general, at all like what was required to make its language intelligible Egyptian; although most of the proper names seemed to exhibit a tolerable agreement with the forms of letters indicated by Mr Åkerblad; a coincidence, indeed, which might be found in the Chinese, or in any other character not alphabetical, if they employed words of the simple sounds for writing compound proper names ... A similar correspondence between the text and the tablets is still more readily observable in other manuscripts, written in distinct hieroglyphics, slightly yet not inelegantly traced, in a hand which appears to have been denoted by the term *hieratic*; and by comparing with each other such parts of the texts of these manuscripts, as stand under tablets of the same kind, we discover, upon a very minute examination, that every character of the distinct hieroglyphics has its corresponding trace in the running hand; sometimes a mere dash or line, but often perfectly distinguishable, as a coarse copy of the original delineation, and always alike when it answers to the same character. The particular passages which establish this identity, extending to a series of above ten thousand characters, have been enumerated in the *Museum Criticum*; they have been copied in adjoining lines, and carefully collated with each other; and their number has been increased, by a comparison with some yet unpublished rolls of papyrus, lately brought from Egypt. A few specimens from different manuscripts will be sufficient to show the forms through which the original representation has passed, in its degradation from the *sacred* character, through the *hieratic*, into the *epistolographic*, or common running hand of the country.

It seems at first sight incomprehensible, that this coincidence, or rather correspondence, should not be equally observable in the two inscriptions of the Rosetta stone, which, if the enchorial character is merely a degradation of the sacred, must naturally be supposed to be as much alike as those of the different manuscripts in question; while, in reality, we can but seldom trace any very striking analogy between them. But the enchorial character, having been long used in rapid writing, and for the ordinary purposes of life, appears to have become so indistinct in its forms, that it was often necessary to add to it some epithet or synonym, serving to mark the object more distinctly: just as, in speaking Chinese, when the words are translated from written characters into a more limited number of sounds, it is often necessary, on account of the imperfection of the oral language, to add a generic word, in order to determine the signification, and to read, for example, *a goose bird*, when *a goose* only is written, in order to distinguish it from some other idea implied by a similar sound; and even in English we might somethimes be obliged to say *a yew tree*, in order to distinguish it from *a ewe sheep*, or *you yourself*, or *the letter u*. The enchorial character, therefore, though drawn from the same source, can scarcely, in this form, be called the same language with the sacred hieroglyphics, which had probably remained unaltered from the earliest ages, while the running hand admitted all the variations of the popular dialects, and bore but a faint resemblance to its original prototype. Indeed, if it had been completely identical, there could have been no propriety in repeating the inscription with so slight a change of form.

The rituals and hymns, contained in the manuscripts which have been mentioned, are probably either of higher antiquity than the inscription of Rosetta, or had preserved a greater purity of character, as having been continually copied from older originals. It is also remarkable, that, in one of these rolls of papyrus, engraved by Denon, the introduction is in the sacred character, and some of the phrases contained in it may be observed to be repeated in the subsequent part of the manuscript, which is in a kind of running hand, though somewhat less degraded than in most other instances.

It was not unnatural to hope, that the comparison of these different manuscripts would have assisted us very materially in tracing back all the enchorial characters to the corresponding hieroglyphics, as far as the parts of the respective inscriptions remain entire, and even in filling up the deficiencies of the sacred characters, where they are wanting; and something has certainly been gained from it with respect to the names of several of the deities; but on account of the differences which had crept in between the forms of the language expressed by the sacred and the cursive characters, the advantage has hitherto been extremely limited. It seems, indeed, to have been a condition inseparable from the whole of this investigation, that its steps should be intricate and laborious, beyond all that could have been imagined from our previous knowledge of the subject; and that, while a number of speculative reasoners have persuaded themselves, at different times, that they were able to read through a hieroglyphical inscription in the most satisfactory manner, beginning at either end, as it might happen, the only monument that has afforded us any real foundations for reasoning on the subject, is more calculated to repress than to encourage our hopes of ever becoming complete masters of the ancient literature of Egypt; although it is unquestionably capable of serving as a key to much important information, with respect to its history and mythology; nor is it by any means impossible, that a careful consideration of other monuments already known, or of such as are now discovered from day to day, may enable us to detect a number of unknown characters, so situated with respect to others, which are already understood, as to carry with them their own interpretation, supported by a degree of evidence far exceeding mere conjecture.

Champollion's lecture

The lecture delivered on 10 May 1831 by Jean-François Champollion inaugurated the course on archaeology at the Collège de France, and was supposed to serve as an introduction to his Grammaire égyptienne, which was published after his death. Here is an extract from that lecture, which summarizes his works, his debates with other researchers and his view of the Rosetta Stone.

The publication of Zoëga's study on the obelisks immediately preceded the French army's conquest of Egypt. This glorious expedition, which was unique in both its political and scientific goals, for scientific commissions accompanied the army's vanguard, lent a strong impetus to archaeological research on the primordial state of the pharaohs' empire. Frenchman whom the love of science had led to share the hazards of this military enterprise acquainted Europe, by means of faithful drawings, with the significance and the prodigious number of Egypt's ancient monuments. At the Emperor Napoleon's command, maps, perspective views and sectional views showing the overall appearance and details of the temples, palaces and tombs, were published in the splendid collection entitled Description de l'Égypte. The scientific world formed, for the first time, an accurate idea of Egyptian civilization and of the inexhaustible wealth of historical documents contained in the countless instructive sculptures that ornament these structures. Science felt more than ever the total lack of positive ideas regarding the Egyptians' graphic system; none the less, the abundance of hieroglyphic texts and monumental inscriptions the French commission collected in Egypt, while making it regret its inability to read them, provided valuable materials for new research on the nature, procedures and various combinations of Egyptian scripts, and moreover, the news of a bilingual monument discovered in Rosetta suddenly awakened in the scientific world the hope that the mysteries of this graphic system would finally be solved.

In August 1799, an officer in the engineering corps attached to the division of our Egyptian army occupying the town of Rosetta, M. Bouchard, found in the excavations carried out in the old fort a rectangular stone of black granite, whose well-polished surface bore three inscriptions in three different scripts. The upper inscription, in large part destroyed or broken, is in hieroglyphic script; the intermediary text is in an *Egyptian cursive* script, and an inscription in Greek language and characters appears on the third and last part of the stone. The translation of this latter text, which contains a decree issued by the priests of Egypt, who had gathered in Memphis to render homage to King Ptolemy Epiphanes, made it completely certain that the two Egyptian inscriptions on the upper part of the stone contained the faithful expression of the same decree in Egyptian language and in two distinct Egyptian scripts, the *sacred script* or hieroglyphics, and the common or *demotic* script.

The discovery of such a monument fully justified great hopes. The possession of Egyptian texts accompanied by their translation in a known language finally established numerous and incontestable points of departure and comparison that might provide a sound way of approaching the Egyptian graphic system through a combined analysis of the two Egyptian inscriptions by making use of the Greek inscription. From this point on, the formation of mere hypotheses had to be abandoned in favour of the search for facts; and Egyptian studies moved forward, albeit slowly, towards positive results.

As early as 1802, a famous scholar, to whom we owe the flourishing state of oriental literature in France, and whose important works have so eminently contributed to disseminating it throughout Europe, M. le baron Silvestre de Sacy, having received a facsimile of the Rosetta monument, examined the demotic text and compared it with the Greek text, and published a summary of his research in a Letter addressed to Count Chaptal, who was then Minister of the interior.

This letter contains the first bases for the deciphering of the intermediary text, by determining the groups of characters corresponding to the proper nouns *Ptolemy*, *Arsinoe*, *Alexander and Alexandria*, which are mentioned on various occasions in the Greek text.

Soon after, M. Ackerblad, a Swedish orientalist distinguished by a highly varied erudition and a deep knowledge of the Coptic language, pursuing the same route as the French scientist, followed his example in comparing the two texts: he published an analysis of the Greek proper names cited in the inscription in *demotic* characters, and at the same time deduced from this analysis a brief alphabet of *demotic* or *popular* Egyptian.

This initial success seemed at first to confirm the hopes aroused by the monument from Rosetta. But Ackerblad, who had been so successful in analysing the Greek proper nouns, had no success when he tried to apply to the reading of the other parts of the demotic inscription the collection of signs whose value he had just observed in the written expression of these Greek proper nouns.

Not supposing, on one hand, that the Egyptians might have been able to write the words of their language while omitting most of the medial vowels, as has always been done by the Hebrews and the Arabs; and on the other hand, not suspecting that many of the signs used in this text might belong to the class of symbolic characters, the Swedish savant, discouraged by his vain attempts, ceased to concern himself with the monument from Rosetta. None the less, the works of MM. de Sacy and Ackerblad had shown that the common script of the ancient Egyptians expressed foreign proper names by means of genuinely *alphabetical* signs.

It would have been very natural to study the hieroglyphic text on the stela from Rosetta first, since it is composed of image-signs or figurative characters with very distinct forms, and to compare it with the Greek text in order to obtain some precise notions regarding the essence of the sacred signs that form the majority of the known Egyptian inscriptions. However, it was only much later that the hieroglyphic text was subjected to research that was serious and judged as such by sound criticism. Scholars were probably dissuaded from concerning themselves with it by the poor condition of this first part of the monument, fractures having caused a large part of the hieroglyphic text to disappear. Had it been intact, this would have spared investigators much groping and countless uncertainties.

This lacuna was far from being suspected by an anonymous author who published in 1804, in Dresden, an alleged *Analyse de l'inscription hiéroglyphique* of the monument found in Rosetta. The author of this work, reviving Father Kircher's mystical symbolism, thought he recognized in the fourteen extant lines of the hieroglyphic inscription (which constitute scarcely half the original inscription) the complete and coherent version of the ideas expressed in the fifty-four lines of the Greek text. This work could not withstand the slightest examination; none the less, it was reprinted by its author, in Florence, as a sort of formal protest against the direction newly given to studies on the hieroglyphics.

The authors of the numerous papers composing the *Description de l'Égypte* concerned themselves with the various kinds of Egyptian scripts only relative to purely material considerations: they published copies of a great number of hieroglyphic monumental inscriptions, as faithfully as was permitted by the novelty of the subject matter and the constantly recurring dangers that then surrounded the courageous explorers who had collected them. They recognized on the original monuments the existence of certain symbolic characters mentioned by Greek authors, but they dealt only in a general way with the questions relative to the nature and combinations of the elementary signs; they rejected the error, which was then rather common, of conflating under a single name the figures depicted in the bas-reliefs and the true hieroglyphs that accompanied them. Finally, the *Description de l'Égypte* provided scholars with excellent facsimiles of Egyptian manuscripts, whether hieroglyphic or hieratic, and – still too late, no doubt, for the progress of paleographic studies – with a copy of the two Egyptian texts on the monument from Rosetta, which were incontestably more accurate than the one that had already been published by the Royal Society in London. Examined in the true interest of the progress of historical knowledge, this great work confirmed that the most precious notions were hidden in the hieroglyphic inscriptions, which were the obligatory ornaments of all Egyptian edifices; but certain deductions prematurely drawn from the examination of astronomical pictures sculpted on the ceilings of several temples led to very serious errors concerning the relative antiquity of the monuments. Temples were attributed to the most ancient periods, that positive facts force us to attribute to the most recent periods; it was even supposed in a way that every monument in the Egyptian style, decorated with hieroglyphic inscriptions, was *ipso facto* earlier than the conquest of Egypt by Cambyses: as if Egypt, which, under Greco-Roman domination, and earlier under the yoke of the Persians themselves, retained most of its political institutions, had suddenly given up its religion and its own scripts, and ceased for more than eight centuries to practise the arts indispensable to its physical existence and to all its moral needs.

English travellers, driven more by a spirit of national rivalry than by scientific interest itself, vainly sought to diminish the importance of the work performed by the French Commission; but its work will for ever remain a worthy monument to our glorious expedition in Egypt, and the useful research of Dr Young will provide England, far better than all these exaggerated criticisms, with a noble role in the progress of Egyptian studies.

This scholar brought to the comparative examination of the three texts on the Rosetta monument a methodical spirit eminently exercised in the most highly complex problems of the physical and mathematical sciences. By a wholly material comparison, he recognized in the still extant portions of the *demotic* inscription of the hieroglyphic inscription, groups of characters corresponding to the words used in the Greek inscription. This work, the result of a very sagacious comparison, finally established some firm ideas regarding the procedures peculiar to the various branches of the Egyptian graphic system and their respective connections; he furnished material proofs for the ancients' assertion concerning the use of *figurative* and *symbolic* characters in hieroglyphic script; but the essential nature of the script, its relationships with the spoken language, the number, essence and combinations of its fundamental elements, remained uncertain, subject to vague hypotheses.

Like the authors of the *Description de l'Égypte*, Dr. Young did not make a sufficiently sharp distinction between the demotic script (that of the second part of the Rosetta monument, also called *enchorial*) and the cursive script used in the non-hieroglyphic papyri, texts that I have since shown to be *hieratic*, that is, belonging to a *priestly script* which is easy to distinguish from the hieroglyphic script by the particular form of the signs, and separated from *demotic or popular script* by even more essential differences.

As for the nature of hieratic and demotic texts, the English scholar adopted in turn two entirely contradictory systems. In 1816, he believed, with the Egyptian Commission, in the *alphabetic nature* of all the signs composing the middle text on the Rosetta monument, and he tried, by means of Ackerblad's alphabet, augmented by several new signs that he supposed to have a fixed value, to determine the reading of 80 groups of demotic characters extracted from the bilingual monument. But in 1819, abandoning altogether the idea of the real existence of genuinely alphabetical signs in the Egyptian graphic system, Dr Young asserted, on the contrary, that demotic script and that on the hieratic papyri belongs, like the primitive script, the *hieroglyphic*, to a system composed of *purely ideographic* characters. However, convinced that most of the proper names mentioned in the demotic text on the Rosetta monument could be subjected to a *kind of reading* using Ackerblad's alphabet, he concluded that the Egyptians, in order to transcribe *foreign proper names* ALONE, made use, like the Chinese, of signs that were truly *ideographic*, but had been diverted from their ordinary expression to make them *accidentally* represent sounds. It was in this conviction that the English scholar tried to analyse two hieroglyphic proper names, that of *Ptolemy* and that of *Berenice*; but this analysis, defective in its principle, led to no results of any kind, not even for the reading of a single one of the proper names sculpted in such abundance on the monuments of Egypt.

The question relating to the elementary nature of the hieroglyphic system thus remained wholly unanswered: did Egptian scripts proceed *ideographically*, or did they express *ideas by notating the sound of words?*

My works have shown that the truth lies precisely between these two extreme hypotheses: that is, they show that the Egyptian graphic system as a whole employed simultaneously *signs of ideas* and *signs of sounds*; that the phonetic characters, which are of the same nature as the letters of our own alphabet, far from being limited to the expression of foreign proper names alone, formed the largest part of Egyptian hieroglyphic, hieratic and demotic texts, representing, by combining with each other, the sounds and articulations of the words peculiar to the spoken Egyptian language.

This fundamental point of fact, which was demonstrated and developed for the first time in 1824 in my work entitled *Précis du système hiéroglyphique*, has been applied to a large number of original monuments and received the most complete and least anticipated confirmation. Sixteen months passed amid the ruins of Upper and Lower Egypt, thanks to the munificence of our government, led to no modification of this principle, whose certainty and admirable fertility I had so many important opportunities to test.

Its application alone allowed me to conduct the *reading* itself of the phonetic portions, which formed in reality at least three-quarters of each hieroglyphic text: from this resulted my full conviction that the ancient Egyptian language differed in no essential way from the language commonly called *Coptic*; that Egyptian words written in hieroglyphic characters on the most ancient monuments of Thebes, and in Greek characters in Coptic books, have an identical value and in general differ only in the absence of certain medial vowels, which were omitted, following the oriental method, in the primitive orthography. The ideographic or symbolic characters, mixed together with the phonetic characters, became more distinct; I was able to grasp the laws governing their combination, and I came to know successively all the grammatical forms and notations expressed in the Egyptian texts, whether *hieroglyphic* or *hieratic*.

Thus the veil covering the intimate nature of the Egyptian graphic system was gradually lifted; the immense amount of material I had collected during my travels in Egypt and in Nubia between the two cataracts, gave me the means of developing these results. One additional duty was still incumbent upon me, that of making the whole extent of my results known to the scholarly world, of demonstrating their importance by that of the new facts that emerged from their application, and of opening a wholly new avenue to the zeal of investigative minds that devote themselves to the advancement of historical studies. The generosity of the king, in appointing me to a chair of archaeology gives me an opportunity to fulfil this duty and to respond, as fully as I can, to these new scientific needs, almost all of which will be enriched by precious documents through a regular and detailed study of Egyptian antiquities.

Chronology

Egyptian script

- The **first hieroglyphic** (from the Greek hieroglyphikos, 'sacred inscriptions') **signs** appeared around 3200 BCE. **Hieratic** (from the Greek hiero, 'sacred, priestly') script, which is a graphic simplification of hieroglyphic script, developed at the same time.
- Two even more simplified cursive scripts, the abnormal hieratic in the south, and the **demotic** (from Greek demotika, 'popular script') in the north, appeared in the seventh century BCE. They replaced the hieratic in all texts connected with everyday life. Little by little, demotic became prevalent throughout the country.
- **Coptic**, the final stage in the development of Egyptian script, emerged in the third century BCE. It is written with Greek characters and seven additional characters borrowed from demotic. Gradually replaced by Arabic, it persisted only as the liturgical language of Egyptian Christians.
- The development of the language during these twenty-six centuries includes several stages. **Old Egyptian** corresponds to the language as it was used for almost five hundred years during the Old Kingdom and the First Intermediate Period (2600–2022 BCE). 'Classical' or **Middle Egyptian** was used during the Middle Kingdom (2060–1785 BCE), and then preserved in a fossilized form

in literature during the first reigns of the Third Dynasty (1550–1350 BCE), and on certain occasions until the end of paganism. **New Egyptian**, which, starting with the period of Akhenaten (1350 BCE), institutionalized the development of the spoken language, was continued in demotic and Coptic, long after the end of the New Kingdom (1069 BCE). Finally, **Ptolemaic** designates the language and hieroglyphic script as they are seen on the walls of the great temples constructed during the last native dynasties and the late Roman Empire (393 BCE–394 CE).

The first tentative steps

1636. Alongside fantastic notions about the hieroglyphs, Athanasius Kircher discovers that Coptic is a survival of the popular language of the ancient Egyptians.

1744. William Warburton suggests that the Egyptians passed from an ideographic script to a phonetic script.

1761. According to the Abbé Barthélemy, the cartouches contain the names of gods or kings.

1785. Charles Joseph de Guignes assumes that the Egyptians did not transcribe certain vowels and that their three scripts – hieroglyphic, hieratic and demotic – were part of the same system.

1797. Jörgen Zoëga asserts that Egyptian writing includes phonetic elements.

The Rosetta Stone

1799
July. Discovery of the stela at Fort Julien.
29 July. Official announcement at the Institut d'Égypte.
Mid-August. Arrival of the Rosetta Stone in Bulak, Cairo's port.

15 September. The *Courrier d'Égypte* reports the discovery.
1800
24 January. Jean-Joseph Marcel makes the first proof-sheets.
Spring. Back in Paris, General Dugua deposits the proof-sheets of the Rosetta Stone at the National Institute.
March–April. In Alexandria's port, the scientists are prevented from departing with the stela.
1801
6 January. Ameilhon presents a French transcription of the Greek inscription to the National Institute in Paris.
September. The Rosetta Stone is seized by the English.
1802
February. The Rosetta Stone arrives in Portsmouth, England. Transfer to the Society of Antiquaries, then to the British Museum.
July. Casts and facsimiles are sent to various European institutions.
4 November. Presentation to the Society of Antiquaries of Stephen Weston's English translation of the Greek inscription.

The Decipherment

1802. Studying the demotic inscription, Silvestre de Sacy isolates groups of signs corresponding to words in the Greek inscription. Åkerblad gives these signs a phonetic value and establishes an 'alphabet'.
7 August 1810. In a paper presented in Grenoble, Jean-François Champollion asserts that the hieroglyphs represented sounds.
1814. The Egyptians did not write all the vowels, Champollion explains in *L'Égypte sous les pharaons*.
1815. Thomas Young publishes a 'conjectural translation' of the demotic inscription on the Rosetta Stone. He identifies groups of hieroglyphic signs corresponding to Greek words.

1819. Young presents the result of his work in the *Supplement to the Encyclopaedia Britannica*, publishing a table of 220 words or hieroglyphic signs. He explains that the Egyptians used signs corresponding to sounds when writing foreign proper names in hieroglyphics.

April 1821. Champollion establishes that hieratic is a simplified form of the hieroglyphics.

1822. Fourth instalment of the *Description de l'Égypte*, in which the Rosetta Stone is reproduced.

27 September 1822. In the *Lettre à M. Dacier*, Champollion, who has been able to read the names of several Greek and Roman rulers, demonstrates the phonetic value of certain hieroglyphs.

1824. In the *Précis du système hiéroglyphique des anciens Égyptiens*, Champollion explains that this script expresses 'sometimes ideas, sometimes sounds'

Later studies

1828–9. Champollion travels in Egypt and tests on site his method of decipherment.

10 May 1831. Champollion gives his inaugural lecture at the Collège de France.

1836–41. Posthumous publication of Champollion's *Grammaire Égyptienne*.

1837. In his *Lettre à M. le professeur Rosellini sur l'alphabet hiéroglyphique*, Lepsius shows that most hieroglyphic signs have more than one consonant, and explains their phonetic complements.

1849–59. Lepsius publishes his *Denkmäler aus Ägypten und Äthiopien*, accompanied by one thousand plates.

May 1866. The bilingual Canopus Decree is found in Tanis. Analysis of this document definitively confirms the method invented by Champollion.

Notes

1 – Fort Julien

1   War archives, quoted by Clément de La Jonquière, *L'expédition d'Égypte*, vol. 2 (Paris, 1899), p. 350.

2   Lieutenant-colonel Théviôte, Archives de l'armée de terre, Armée d'Orient, Sous-série B6, 'Mémoires historiques', p. 581.

3   Labib Habachi, *Annales du Service des Antiquités de l'Égypte*, 42 (Cairo, 1943), pp. 376–8.

4   Jacques Laurens, 'Pierre Bouchard (1771–1822)', *La Rouge et la Jaune* (journal of the alumni of the École polytechnique), April 1991.

5   Jean-Édouard Goby, *Premier Institut d'Égypte*, Mémoires de l'Académie des inscriptions et belles-lettres, VII (Paris: Institut de France, 1987).

2 – The thirty-first session

1   Jean-Édouard Goby, 'La composition du premier Institut d'Égypte', *Bulletin de l'Institut d'Égypte*, 29 (Cairo, 1948).

2   Abd-al-Rahman al-Jabarti, *Journal d'un notable du Caire durant l'Éxpédition française, 1798–1801*, translated and annotated by Joseph Cuocq (Paris: Albin Michel, 1979).

3   *La Décade égyptienne*, vol. 3, Cairo, year VIII of the Republic

(1800), pp. 293–4.

4   Captain Bouchard, *La Chute d'El-Arich (décembre 1799)*, preface and annotations by Gaston Wiet (Cairo: Éditions de la *Revue du Caire*, 1945).

3 – Sacred signs and symbols

1   *Rerum gestarum libri XXXI*, book XVII, chap. iv.

2   *Histories*, book II, chap. 36.

3   *Bibliotheca historica*, book I, 81. English translation as *Diodorus of Sicily*, trans. C. H. Oldfather (London: 1933, p. 277).

4   *Metamorphoses*, trans. J. Arthur Hanson (Cambridge, Mass. and London: 1989), vol. 2, pp. 337–8.

5   'Isis and Osiris', in Plutarch, *Moralia*, trans. Frank Cole Babbitt (Cambridge, Mass. and London: 1936), vol. V, p. 6.

6   *Chronology of Ancient Kingdoms Amended*, 1728.

7   2 vols., London, 1737–41.

8   *De usu et origine obeliscorum*. Rome, 1797.

4 – With the point of a compass

1   Louis Reybaud et al., *Histoire scientifique et militaire de l'Éxpédition française en Égypte*, (Paris, 1830–36), vol. VI, pp. 440–41.

2   *Ibid.*, p. 442.

3   Quoted by Prosper Jollois in *Journal d'un ingénieur attaché à l'Expédition d'Égypte (1798–1802)* (Paris: Ernest Leroux, 1904).

5 – The spoils of war

1 Captain Bouchard, Journal du siège du Fort Julien, Archives de l'armée de terre, Armée d'Orient, Sous-série BC, 'Mémoires historiques', p. 552.
2 Jacques Laurens, 'Pierre Bouchard (1771–1822)', La Rouge et la Jaune (journal of the alumni of the École polytechnique), April 1991.
3 Quoted by François Rousseau, Kléber et Menou en Égypte (Paris, 1900).
4 Ibid.
5 Robert Thomas Wilson, History of the British Expedition to Egypt (London: T. Egerton, 1803), vol. 2.
6 Archives de la Guerre, quoted by Paul Pallary in Marie Jules César Savigny, sa vie et son oeuvre (Cairo: IFAO, 1931–4), vol. 1.
7 This letter and the following ones are reproduced by Paul Pallary, op. cit.
8 Louis Reybaud et al., Histoire scientifique et militaire de l'Expédition française en Égypte, (Paris, 1830–36), vol. VIII, p. 419.
9 Ibid., p. 421.
10 Aegyptiaca (London, 1809).
11 Letter to the secretary of the Society of Antiquaries, reproduced in Archaeologia, vol. XVI, Society of Antiquaries of London (London, 1812), pp. 212 ff.
12 Archives nationales, F17 1101, dossier 3.

6 – King George's gift

1 Matthew Roper, 'An Account of the Rosetta Stone', in Archaeologia, London, vol. XVI (1812).
2 Harry James, 'The development of the Egyptian collection in the British Museum', in L'Egitto fuori dell'Egitto (Clueb, Bologna).

3   Éclaircissements sur l'inscription grecque du monument trouvé à Rosette (Paris, floréal an IX [1803]).

4   Jean-Antoine Letronne, Inscription grecque de Rosette, texte et traduction littérale, accompagnée d'un commentaire critique, historique et archéologique (1841).

7 – Description, for want of something better

1   Yves Laissus, L'Égypte, une aventure savante (Paris: Fayard, 1998), p. 472.
2   'Antiquités', in Description de l'Égypte, (Paris, 1809–28), vol. V, plates 53–54.
3   Ibid., plate 52.
4   Edme François Jomard, Souvenirs sur Gaspard Monge (Paris, 1853).
5   'Antiquités,' 'Explication des planches', in Description de l'Égypte, op. cit., vol. V, p. 548.
6   Ibid., p. 547.
7   Ibid., vol. IX, 'Antiquités', 'Mémoires et descriptions', p. 574.

8 – Åkerblad's 'alphabet'

1   Antoine Isaac Silvestre de Sacy, Lettre au citoyen Chaptal au sujet de l'inscription égyptienne du monument trouvé à Rosette (Paris, 1802).
2   Åkerblad, Johann David, Lettre sur l'inscription égyptienne de Rosette, adressée au citoyen Silvestre de Sacy (Paris, 1802).
3   Letter to Thomas Young, quoted in Miscellaneous Works of the Late Thomas Young, vol.III, Hieroglyphical Essays and Correspondence, etc. ed. John Leitch (London, 1855), pp. 30–4.
4   Ibid., p. 17.

9 – Champollion goes to work

1   Jean Lacouture, *Champollion; une vie de lumières* (Paris: Grasset, 1988).

2   Hermine Hartleben, *Jean-François Champollion: sa vie et son œuvre 1790–1832*, French trans. (Paris: Pygmalion, 1983), pp. 47–8.

3   Jean-François Champollion, *Lettres à son frère*, presented by Pierre Vaillant (Paris: L'Asiathèque, 1984), pp. 5–7.

4   Bibliothèque municipale de Grenoble, R 7590.

5   Jean-François Champollion, *Lettres à son frère*, op. cit., p. 75.

6   Ibid., pp. 26–9.

7   *Miscellaneous Works of the Late Thomas Young*, vol. III, *Hieroglyphical essays and correspondence*, etc., ed. John Leitch (London, 1855), p. 17.

8   Johann David Åkerblad, *Lettre sur l'inscription égyptienne de Rosette, adressée au citoyen Silvestre de Sacy* (Paris, 1802).

9   Étienne Quatremère, *Recherches critiques et historiques sur la langue et la littérature de l'Égypte* (Paris, 1808).

10 Id., *Mémoires géographiques et historiques sur l'Égypte et sur quelques contrées voisines recueillis et extraits des manuscrits coptes, arabes, etc., de la Bibliotheque imperiale* (Paris, 1811).

11 Id., *Observation sur quelques points de la géographie de l'Égypte* (see Hermine Hartleben, *Jean-François Champollion: sa vie et son œuvre 1790–1832*, French trans. (Paris: Pygmalion, 1983), p. 124.

12 Quoted by Jean Leclant, 'Champollion, la pierre de Rosette et le déchiffrement des hiéroglyphes', Académie des inscriptions et belles-lettres (Paris, 1972), p. 7.

13 Jean-François Champollion, *L'Égypte sous le pharaons ou Recherches sur la géographie, la religion, la langue, les écritures et l'histoire de l'Égypte avant l'invasion de Cambyse* (Paris, 1814).

14 Ibid., p. 87 (Ptah), p. 105 (Kémy), etc.

15 Letter to Thomas Young, in *Miscellaneous Works of the Late Thomas Young*, op. cit., p. 17.

10 – Signed 'ABCD'

1   *Miscellaneous Works of the Late Thomas Young*, vol. III,
    Hieroglyphical Essays and Correspondence, etc., ed. John Leitch
    (London, 1855), p. 16.

2   Ibid., pp. 17–18.

3   *Archaeologia*, vol. VIII: *Remarks on Egyptian Papyri, and on the
    Inscription of Rosetta (Containing an Interpretation of the
    Principal Parts of Both the Egyptian Inscriptions on the Pillar)*.

4   Thomas Young, 'An Account of Some Recent Discoveries
    in Hieroglyphical Literature and Egyptian Antiquities
    Including the Author's Alphabet, as Extended by Mr
    Champollion with a Translation of Five Unpublished
    Greek and Egyptian Manuscripts' (1823), in *Miscellaneous
    Works of the Late Thomas Young*, op. cit., pp. 12–13.

5   Ibid., pp. 49–52.

6   *Museum Criticum of Cambridge*, vol. VI (1816).

7   *Miscellaneous Works of the Late Thomas Young*, op. cit., pp.
    74–85. These two letters were published in the *Museum
    Criticum*, vol. VII, whose publication was delayed until
    1821 although printed copies were in circulation as early
    as 1816.

8   See appendix III.

9   *Miscellaneous Works of the Late Thomas Young*, op. cit., p. 58.

10 Thomas Young, 'An Account...', op. cit., p. 14.

11 Jean-François Champollion, *Précis du système hiéroglyphique
    des anciens Égyptiens ou Recherches sur les éléments de cette
    écriture sacrée, sur leurs diverses combinaisons, et sur les rapports
    de ce système avec les autres méthodes graphiques égyptiennes*
    Paris, 1824), p. 8.

11 – Three related scripts

1   Jean Leclant, 'L'histoire de l'Académie des inscriptions et

belles-lettres', extract from *Histoire des cinq académies* (Paris: Perrin, 1995), pp. 109, 117, 124–5.

2   *Miscellaneous Works of the Late Thomas Young*, vol. III, *Hieroglyphical Essays and Correspondence, etc.*, ed. John Leitch (London, 1855), pp. 62–4.

3   Ibid., pp. 64–5.

4   Ibid., pp. 65–6.

5   Jean-François Champollion, *Lettres à son frère*, presented by Pierre Vaillant (Paris: L'Asiathéque, 1984), pp. 41–3.

6   Ibid., pp. 51–2.

7   *De l'écriture hiératique des anciens Égyptiens* (Grenoble, 1821).

12 – The letter to M. Dacier

1   Paper presented to the Académie des inscriptions et belles-lettres, 31 August and 7 September 1821.

2   *Miscellaneous Works of the Late Thomas Young*, vol. III, *Hieroglyphical Essays and Correspondence, etc.*, ed. John Leitch (London, 1855), pp. 51, 59.

3   Jean-François Champollion, *Précis du système hiéroglyphique des anciens Égyptiens ou recherches sur les éléments de cette écriture sacrée, sur leurs diverses combinaisons, et sur les rapports de ce systéme avec les autres méthodes graphiques égyptiennes* (Paris, 1824), pp. 266–8.

4   'Observations sur l'obélisque égyptien de l'île de Philae', *Revue encyclopédique*, vol. XIII (March 1822), pp. 512–21.

5   Charles-Olivier Carbonell, 'Jacques-Joseph et Jean-François Champollion, la naissance d'un génie', *Bulletin de la Société française d'égyptologie*, vol. 65 (1972), pp. 36–8.

6   Manuscript register of the meetings of the Académie royale des inscriptions et belles-lettres, p. 405.

7   Published in the *Journal des savants* (Paris: October, 1822), pp. 620–28 and plate 1.

13 – Ideas and sounds

1   Jean Leclant, 'Champollion, la pierre de Rosette et le
    déchiffrement des hiéroglyphes,' (Paris: Académie des
    inscriptions et belles-lettres, 1972), p. 11.
2   In French in the text. The first step is the hardest.
3   *Miscellaneous Works of the Late Thomas Young*, vol. III,
    Hieroglyphical Essays and Correspondence, etc., ed. John Leitch
    (London, 1855), pp. 220–23.
4   Ibid., pp. 244–6.
5   *An Account of Some Recent Discoveries in Hieroglyphical
    Literature and Egyptian Antiquities ...*, p. 51.
6   Letter to W. Gell, in *Miscellaneous Works of the Late Thomas
    Young*, op. cit., p. 370.
7   Thomas Young, *Hieroglyphics, Collected by the Egyptian
    Society* (London, 1823; rpt. Wiesbaden, 1982).

14 – A science is born

1   Edward Clarke, *Travels in Various Countries of Europe and
    Africa* (London, 1814), vol. 3, II, 'Greece, Egypt', pp. 46–7.
2   Exchange of letters, in *Miscellaneous Works of the Late
    Thomas Young*, vol. III, *Hieroglyphical Essays and
    Correspondence, etc.*, ed. John Leitch (London, 1855), pp.
    67–9.
3   Thomas Young, *Hieroglyphics*, collected by the Egyptian
    Society (London, 1823; rpt., Wiesbaden, 1982).
4   Auriant, *Bataille d'égyptologues autour d'une stèle* (rpt.,
    Rheims, A l'écart, 1978).
5   *Miscellaneous Works of the Late Thomas Young*, op. cit., p. 433.
6   It appeared in the first edition of Emmanuel de Rougé's
    Notice des monuments égyptiens, under the number C 122.
7   Letter to John Baker, 17 April 1829, in *Collectanea*, British
    Museum, folio 42.

15 – Decipherers by the hundreds

1   Nils Gustav Palin, *Essai sur les hiéroglyphes* (Weimar, 1804); *Analyse de l'inscription en hiéroglyphes du monument trouvé à Rosette* (Dresden, 1804).

2   *Miscellaneous Works of the Late Thomas Young*, vol. III, *Hieroglyphical Essays and Correspondence, etc.*, ed. John Leitch (London, 1855), p. 72.

3   Jean-François Champollion, *Lettres à son frère*, presented by Pierre Vaillant (Paris: L'Asiat Légue, 1984), p. 41.

4   'Lettre à M. le Rédacteur de la *Revue encyclopédique* relative au zodiaque de Dendéra', *Revue encyclopédique*, vol. XVI (August 1802), pp. 232–9. Offprints of this article were circulated.

5   Alexandre Lenoir, *Nouvelle Explication des hiéroglyphes ou des anciennes allégories sacrées des Égyptiens, utile à l'intelligence des monuments mythologiques des autres peuples* (Paris, 1809–21).

6   James Bailey, *Hieroglyphicorum origo et natura* (Cambridge, 1816).

7   Pierre Lacour, *Essai sur les hiéroglyphes* (Bordeaux, 1821).

8   Jean-François Champollion, 'Lettre de M. Champollion le Jeune à Monsieur Z****', extract from the journal *Memorie Romane d'antichità e belle arti*, vol. I (Rome, 1825).

9   Champollion le Jeune, 'Sur la découverte des hiéroglyphes acrologiques adressée à M. le chev. de Goulianoff, par M. Klaproth (1 vol. in 80, Paris, 1827). Analyse critique de cet ouvrage', extract from the *Bulletin universel des sciences*, VIIth section (April 1827), pp. 1–11.

10 Id., *Lettre à M. le duc de Blacas d'Aulps, premier gentilhomme de la Chambre, pair de France, etc., sur le nouveau système hiéroglyphique de MM. Spohn et Seyffarth* (Florence, 1826).

11 Henry Salt, *Essai sur le système des hiéroglyphes phonétiques du Dr Young et de M. Champollion* (London, 1825). Reviewed by Jean-François Champollion in *Bulletin universel des sciences*, VIIth section (January 1826).

12 Quoted by Hermine Hartleben, *Jean-François Champollion: sa vie et son œuvre 1790–1832* (Paris: Pygmalion, 1983), pp. 266–7.

13 François Arago, 'Sur l'écriture hiéroglyphique égyptienne', in *Fragment de l'éloge historique du Dr Thomas Young* (Paris, 1832).

14 An extensive bibliography on this subject can be found in J. Kettel, *Jean-François Champollion le Jeune, Répertoire de bibliographie analytique (1806–1989)*, Mémoire de l'Académie des inscriptions et belles-lettres (Paris, 1990).

15 *Annali dell'Istituto di corrispondenza archeologica*, vol. IX, part 1 (1837), pp. 5–100.

16 Karl Richard Lepsius, *Denkmäler aus Ägypten und Äthiopien* (Berlin, 1849–59).

17 Id., *Das bilingue Dekret von Kanopus in der Originalgrösse mit Übersetzung beider Texte* (Berlin, 1866).

18 François Chabas, *Voyage d'un Égyptien en Syrie, en Phénicie, en Palestine …* (Paris, 1866).

19 Heinrich Karl Brugsch, *Grammaire hiéroglyphique contenant les principes généraux de la langue et de l'écriture sacrée des anciens Égyptiens composée à l'usage des étudiants* (Leipzig, 1872).

20 Victor Loret, *Manuel de la langue égyptienne, grammaire, tableau des hiéroglyphes, textes et glossaires* (Paris, 1889).

21 Adolf Erman, *Neuägyptische Grammatik mit Schrifttafel, Literatur, Lesestücken und Wörterverzeichnis* (Berlin, 1894).

16 – The magic of a script

1 Serge Sauneron, ed., *Textes et Langages de l'Égypte pharaonique (Hommage à Jean-François Champollion)*, Bibliothèque d'étude 64/1-3 (Cairo: IFAO, 1972).

17 – The fate of a stone

1 Christiane Desroches-Noblecourt, *La Grande Nubiade ou le parcours d'une égyptologue* (Paris: Stock-Pernoud, 1992).
2 *The Times*, 20 October 1972.
3 Quoted in *The Egyptian Gazette*, 18 December 1993.

Appendix 1 – The Memphis Decree

1 Wilhelm Spiegelberg, *Der demotische Text der Priesterdekrete von Kanopus und Memphis (Rosettana)* (Heidelberg, 1922).
2 Philippe Derchain, *Le Dernier Obélisque* (Brussels: Fondation égyptologique Reine-Élisabeth, 1987).

Appendix II – Other bilingual stelae

1 Henri Gauthier, 'À travers la Basse-Égypte,' ASAE 23, pp. 170–71; André Bernand, *La Prose sur pierre dans l'Égypte hellénistique et romaine* (Paris: CNRS, 1992), vol. I, pp. 50–53; vol. II, p. 54.
2 Henri Sottas, *Sur trois fragments d'un double de la pierre de Rosette provenant d'Éléphantine*, Académie des inscriptions et belles-lettres, vol. XIII, pt. 2 (Paris, 1933), pp. 485–505; André Bernand, op. cit., vol. I, pp. 54–7; vol. 2, pp. 55–6; François Daumas, *Les Moyens d'expression du grec et de l'égyptien comparés dans les décrets de Canope et de Memphis* (Cairo: IFAO, 1952), pp. 6–7.
3 Kurt Sethe, *Zur Geschichte und Erklärung der Rosettana* (Klasse, 1916), pp. 275–314; François Daumas, *Les Moyens d'expression du grec et de l'égyptien ...,* op. cit., pp. 6–7.
4 Ibid., pp. 7–8.
5 Bouché-Leclerq, *Histoire des Lagides*, vol. I.
6 François Daumas, *Notions générales sur les décrets de Canope et*

de Memphis, CASAE 16 (Cairo: Egyptian Antiquities Service, 1952).

7   Serge Sauneron, 'Un cinquième exemplaire du décret de Canope', *Bulletin de l'Institut français d'archéologie orientale*, 56 (1957), pp. 67–75 and plate 1.

8   Jean Lauffray, Serge Sauneron, Ramadan Saad and Pierre Anus, 'Rapport sur les travaux de Karnak. Activités du Centre franco-égyptien en 1968–1969', *Kêmi*, 20 (1970), pp. 73–4.

Bibliography

The hieroglyphs before the discovery of the Rosetta Stone

Chauveau, Michel. *L'Égypte au temps de Cléopatre (180–30 av. J.-C.)*. Paris: Hachette Littératures, 1997.

Donadoni, Sergio, Curto, Silvio, and Donadoni Roveri, Anna Maria. *L'Égypte, du mythe à l'égyptologie*. Milan, 1990.

Froidefond, Christian. *Le Mirage égyptien dans la littérature grecque d'Homère à Aristote*. Aix-en-Provence: Université Aix-Marseille I, 1971.

Iversen, Erik. *The Myth of Egypt and its Hieroglyphs*. Princeton University Press, 1961; rpt. 1993.

Marestaing, Pierre. *Les Écritures égyptiennes et l'Antiquité classique*. Paris, 1913.

Works by classical authors dealing with hieroglyphs

Ammianus Marcellinus. *Rerum gestarum libri XXXI*. Book XVII. Trans. John Rolfe. Cambridge, Mass. and London: Loeb Classical Library, Harvard University Press and Heinemann, 1935, vol. I.

Apuleius, *Metamorphoses*. Trans. J. Arthur Hanson. Cambridge, Mass. and London: Loeb Classical Library, Harvard University Press, 1989. Book XI.

Diodorus Siculus (Diodorus of Sicily). *Bibliotheca historica*.
Book I. Trans. C. H. Oldfather as *Diodorus of Sicily*.
London: Loeb Classical Library, Heinemann, 1933–67.

Horapollo. *Hieroglyphica*. Trans. G. Boas. New York: Bollingen
Series XXIII, 1950.

Jamblichus. *De Mysteriis*. Text and French translation E. Des
Places. 1966.

Plato. *Philebus*. In *The Collected Dialogues of Plato*. Ed. Edith
Hamilton and Huntington Cairns. Princeton: Bollingen
Series LXXI, 1961.

Plotinus. *Enneads V*, Trans. A. H. Armstrong. Cambridge,
Mass. And London: Loeb Classical Library, 1966–88.

Plutarch. *Moralia*. 'Isis and Osiris', trans. Frank Cole Babbitt.
Cambridge, Mass. and London: Loeb Classical Library,
Harvard University Press, 1936, vol. V.

Porphyry. *Vie de Pythagore*. French translation E. Des Places, 1982.

Tacitus. *Annal,s XI. The Annals of Imperial Rome*, tr. Michael
Grant, new edition. Harmondsworth: Penguin, 1996.

Works written during the Renaissance and Modern Times

Kircher, Athanasius. *Prodomus coptus sive aegyptiacus*. 1636.
— . *Œdipus aegyptiacus*. 1652–4.
— . *Sphynx mystagoga*. 1676.
Warburton, William. *Essay on the Egyptian Hieroglyphs*. Paris,
1744 (new edition, Paris Aubier-Montaigne, 1978).

The French expedition to Egypt

*Description de l'Égypte ou Recueil des observations et des recherches qui
ont été faites en Égypte pendant l'Expédition de l'armée française*.
Paris, 1809–28. 9 vols. plus 11 vols. of plates; rpt., Paris,

Panckoucke, 1821–30, 26 vols. plus 11 vols. of plates.

La Jonquière, Clément de. *L'Expédition d'Égypte*. Paris, 1899–1907. 5 vols.

Meulenaere, Philippe de. *Bibliographie raisonnée des témoignages oculaires imprimés de l'Expédition d'Égypte (1798–1801)*. Paris: Chamonal, 1993.

Munier, Henri. *Tables de la 'Description de l'Égypte'*. Cairo, 1936.

Reybaud, Louis, et al. *Histoire scientifique et militaire de l'Expédition française en Égypte*. Paris, 1830–36. 10 vols.

Turner, Tomkins Hilgrave. 'Letter to the Secretary of the Society of Antiquaries'. Reproduced in *Archaeologia*, London, vol. XVI (1812), pp. 212.

The beginning of the decipherment

Åkerblad, Johann David. *Lettre sur l'inscription égyptienne de Rosette, adressée au citoyen Silvestre de Sacy*. Paris, 1802.

Ameilhon. *Éclaircissements sur l'inscription grecque du monument trouvé à Rosette*. Paris, floréal an IX (1803).

Roper, Matthew. 'An Account of the Rosetta Stone'. *Archaeologia*, London, vol. XVI (1812).

Silvestre de Sacy, Antoine Isaac. *Lettre au citoyen Chaptal au sujet de l'inscription égyptienne du monument trouvé à Rosette*. Paris, 1802.

Thomas Young

Bibliography and correspondence

Miscellaneous Works of the Late Thomas Young. vol. III, *Hieroglyphical Essays and Correspondence, etc.* John Leitch, ed. London, 1855.

Gurney, Hudson. *Memoir of the Life of Thomas Young*. London, 1831.

Wood, Alexander, and Oldham, Frank. *Thomas Young.* Cambridge, 1954.

Works by Young

'Egypt.' In *Encyclopaedia Britannica.* 1819.

Museum Criticum of Cambridge VI. 1816.

Museum Criticum of Cambridge VII. 1821.

An Account of Some Recent Discoveries in Hieroglyphical Literature[1] *and Egyptian Antiquities Including the Author's original Alphabet, as Extended by Mr. Champollion, with a Translation of Five Unpublished Greek and Egyptian Manuscripts.* London, 1823.

Hieroglyphics, Collected by the Egyptian Society. London, 1823. Rpt., Wiesbaden, 1982.

Jean-François Champollion

Bibliography

Kettel, Jeannot. *Jean-François Champollion le Jeune: répertoire de bibliographie analytique 1806–1989.* Paris: Académie des inscriptions et belles-lettres, 1989.

Biography, correspondence, documents

Champollion, Jean-François, *Lettres à son frère.* Presented by Pierre Vaillant. Paris: L'Asiathèque, 1984.

— . *Lettres écrites d'Égypte et de Nubie en 1828 et 1829.* Paris, 1833.

Champollion-Figeac, Aimé. *Les deux Champollions. Leur vie et leurs œuvres, leur correspondance archéologique relative au Dauphiné et à l'Égypte.* Grenoble, 1887.

Hartleben, Hermine. *Jean-François Champollion: sa vie et son œuvre 1790–1832.* Paris: Pygmalion, 1983.

Lacouture, Jean. *Champollion; une vie de lumières.* Paris: Grasset, 1988.

Leclant, Jean. 'Champollion, la pierre de Rosette et le

déchiffrement des hiéroglyphes'. Paris: Académie des inscriptions et belles-lettres, 1972.

Champollion's main works

L'Égypte sous les pharaons ou Recherches sur la géographie, la religion, la langue, les écritures et l'histoire de l'Égypte avant l'invasion de Cambyse. Paris, 1814.

Lettre à M. Dacier, secrétaire perpétuel de l'Académie royale des inscriptions et belles-lettres relative à l'alphabet des hiéroglyphes phonétiques employés par les Égyptiens pour inscrire sur leurs monuments les titres, les noms, et les surnoms des souverains grecs et romains. Paris, 1822; rpt., Fata Morgana, 1989.

Panthéon égyptien. Paris, 1823–25.

Précis du système hiéroglyphique des anciens Égyptiens ou Recherches sur les éléments de cette écriture sacrée, sur leurs diverses combinaisons, et sur les rapports de ce système avec les autres méthodes graphiques égyptiennes. Paris, 1824; 2nd ed. 1828.

Grammaire égyptienne ou Principes généraux de l'écriture sacrée égyptienne appliquée à la représentation de la langue parlée. Paris, 1836; rpt. Solin-Actes Sud, 1997.

Writers who sought to decipher Egyptian scripts

Bailey, James. Hieroglyphicorum origo et natura. Cambridge, 1816.

Lacour, Pierre. Essai sur les hiéroglyphes. Bordeaux, 1821.

Lenoir, Alexandre. Nouvelle Explication des hiéroglyphes ou des anciennes allégories sacrées des Égyptiens, utile à l'intelligence des monuments mythologiques des autres peuples. Paris, 1809–21.

Palin, Nils Gustav. Essai sur les hiéroglyphes. Weimar, 1804.

— . Analyse de l'inscription en hiéroglyphes du monument trouvé à Rosette. Dresden, 1804.

Quatremère, Étienne. Recherches critiques et historiques sur la langue et la littérature de l'Égypte. Paris, 1808.

———. *Mémoires géographiques et historiques sur l'Égypte et sur quelques contrées voisines recueillies et extraits des manuscrits coptes, arabes, etc., de la Bibliothèque impériale.* Paris, 1811.

Egyptian language, script and grammar

Brugsch, Heinrich Karl. *Grammaire hiéroglyphique contenant les principes généraux de la langue et de l'écriture sacrée des anciens Égyptiens composée à l'usage des étudiants.* Leipzig, 1872.

Černý, Jaroslav, and Sarah Groll. *A Late Egyptian Grammar.* Rome, 1975.

Edel, Elmar. *Altägyptische Grammatik.* Rome, 1955–64.

Erman, Adolf. *Neuägyptische Grammatik mit Schrifttafel Literatur, Lesestücken und Wörterverzeichnis.* Berlin, 1894; rpt. Hildesheim, 1968.

Gardiner, Alan Henderson. *Egyptian Grammar.* 3rd edition: Oxford, 1957.

Grandet, Pierre, and Bernard Mathieu, *Cours d'égyptien hiéroglyphique.* Paris: Khéops, 1997.

Kahl, J. *Das System der ägyptischen Hieroglyphenscrift in der O.-3. Dynastie.* Wiesbaden, 1994.

Lefebvre, Gustave. *Grammaire de l'égyptien classique.* Paris, 2nd ed. rev. and corr. by Serge Sauneron, 1955.

Lepsius, Karl Richard. *Denkmäler aus Ägypten und Äthiopien.* 12 vols. Berlin, 1849–59.

———. *Das bilingue Dekret von Kanopus in der Originalgrösse mit Übersetzung beider Texte.* Berlin, 1866.

Loret, Victor. *Manuel de la langue égyptienne, grammaire, tableau des hiéroglyphiques, textes et glossaires.* Paris, 1889.

Neveu, François. *La Langue des Ramsès. Grammaire du néo-égyptien.* Paris: Khéops, 1996.

Sauneron, Serge, ed. *Textes et Langages de l'Égypte pharaonique (Hommage à Jean-François Champollion).* Bibliothèque d'étude 64. Cairo: IFAO, 1972.

The Rosetta Stone and the bilingual decrees

Andrews, Carol. *The Rosetta Stone*. London: British Museum, 1982.

—, and Quirke, S., *The Rosetta Stone: Facsimile Drawing*. London: British Museum, 1988.

Bernand, André. *La Prose sur pierre dans l'Égypte hellénistique et romaine*. 2 vols. Paris: CNRS, 1992.

Bernand, Étienne. *Inscriptions grecques d'Égypte et de Nubie. Répertoire bibliographique des 16RR*. Paris: Les Belles Lettres, 1983, no. 90, pp. 24–5.

Budge, E. A. Wallis. *The Decrees of Memphis and Canopus*. 3 vols. London, 1904.

—. *The Rosetta Stone*. London, 1913.

Daumas, François. *Les Moyens d'expression du grec et de l'égyptien comparés dans les décrets de Canope et de Memphis*. Cahier des Annales du Service des Antiquités de l'Égypte, 16, Cairo, 1952.

—. 'Les textes bilingues ou trilingues', in Serge Sauneron, ed., *Textes et Langages de l'Égypte pharaonique* (Hommage à Jean-François Champollion). Bibliothèque d'étude 64. Cairo: IFAO, 1972.

Devauchelle, Didier. *La Pierre de Rosette. Présentation et traduction*. Paris: Le Léopard d'or, 1990.

Lauffray, Jean, Serge Sauneron, Ramadan Saad, and Pierre Anus. 'Rapport sur les travaux de Karnak. Activités du Centre franco-égyptien en 1968–1969.' *Kêmi*, 20, 1970.

Revillout, Eugène. 'Les deux versions hiéroglyphiques du décret de Rosette, accompagnés du texte démotique transcrit en hiéroglyphes et de la version grecque.' *Revue égyptologique*, XIII, pp. 43–108.

Sauneron, Serge. 'Un cinquième exemplaire du décret de Canope', *Bulletin de l'Institut français d'archéologie orientale*, 56, 1957.

Sethe, Kurt. *Zur Geschichte und Erklärung der Rosettana*. Klasse,

1916, pp. 275–314.

Sottas, Henri. *Sur trois fragments d'un double de la pierre de Rosette provenant d'Éléphantine.* Paris: Académie des inscriptions et belles-lettres, vol. XIII, pt. 2, 1933. pp. 485–505.

Spiegelberg, Wilhelm. *Der demotische Text der Priesterdekrete von Kanopus und Memphis (Rosettana).* Heidelberg, 1922.

Thissen, H.-J. 'Rosette, Stein von'. *Lexikon der Ägyptologie.* Wiesbaden: Otto Harrassowitz, 1984, vol. V, cols. 310–11.

Index of names